The Valiant Woman

THE VALIANT WOMAN

A Series of Discourses Intended
For the Use of Women Living in the World

By
Monseigneur Landriot,
Archbishop of Rheims,
(Formerly Bishop of La Rochelle)
Translated from the French by Helena Lyons

Loreto Publications
Fitzwilliam, New Hampshire
A.D. 2005

Originally published by Marlier Publishing Company, Boston.

Typesetting, Layout, Cover design
copyright 2005 Loreto Publications.
All rights reserved.

ISBN: 1-930278-39-X

Published by:
Loreto Publications
P. O. Box 603 • Fitzwilliam, N.H. 03447
Phone: 603-239-6671
Fax: 603-239-6127
www.LoretoPubs.org

Printed and bound in the United States of America

Preface

It is sometimes said that current English literature contains more than a fair proportion of exclusively imaginative works. The undersigned desires to offer, as a humble contribution in the opposite direction, the translation of a book which has done useful service in France, and which she hopes may not be without some practical utility among her own fair countrywomen. *La Femme Forte*, or, as translated, *The Valiant Woman*, by Monseigneur Landriot, now Archbishop of Rheims, is more especially addressed to married women, but is replete with useful lessons for the unmarried also. It is a common complaint that there are, among the married, women who entertain a notion that domestic life and attention to home duties are not the natural sphere of action for a wife; but, on the contrary, her business is to participate in the gaieties and frivolities of the world of pleasure. The lessons to be derived from the translation now offered to the public are: that woman's proper sphere is her home; her chief happiness is to be found in the discharge of her domestic duties; that she has it in her power to diffuse light and culture, by the practice of virtues peculiarly belonging to the sex; and that on her, in great measure, rests the responsibility of training the rising generation, and materially affecting the happiness and prosperity of the country, by moulding the plastic character of its youth. The lessons here taught further show wherein lie the real rights and privileges of women; and, by doing so, serve to warn them against striving after objects more showy in appearance, but less noble in their aim.

That so blessed a consummation may be effected, is the one wish of,

THE TRANSLATOR

Editor's Preface to the Fourth Edition

These discourses, which explain from Holy Scripture some of the principal duties of Christian women living in the world, are taken from the instructions which the Bishop of La Rochelle gives every month to the ladies of the Society of Charity established in his episcopal city.

The style, character, and details suitable for familiar instruction have been preserved in these discourses, which were not written for publication.

It is proposed to publish later the continuation of these conferences, which were specially intended for women living in the world, and which point out to them the rules of true piety.[1]

The first three editions were exhausted in less than a year. This is the best proof of the favorable reception of *The Valiant Woman*.

In publishing this Fourth Edition, we believe we are corresponding with the wishes of those who are able to appreciate the lessons of lofty Christian philosophy given by the learned Bishop of La Rochelle.

---

[1] This project has been already begun by the publication of *La Femme Pieuse*, or "The Pious Woman."

Publisher's Dedication

This 21ˢᵗ century edition of The Valiant Woman is dedicated to my wife Kathleen who discovered this long out of print title and brought it to my attention. She has made this book "her own" and has derived much fruit from her many readings of it, as have I.

The Holy Ghost poses the question, "Who shall find a valiant woman?" I am delighted and profoundly thankful to be able to answer that I have. To the one that I have found, with joy and deepest affection, I dedicate this publication.

It is a small token of my gratitude to God for being truly able to answer this question as I have, that I present to the public, hungry to learn the art of practical virtue, this new edition of Msgr. Landriot's classic. It is my hope that it may benefit the reader as much as it has benefited myself.

TABLE OF CONTENTS

Preface v

Editor's Preface to the Fourth Edition vii

First Discourse: A portrait of the Valiant Woman...............1

Second Discourse: The Valiant Woman reigns over one empire, and that is her home. 13

Third Discourse: Prudence in balancing the domestic economy with other healthy pursuits.................................23

Fourth Discourse : The Valiant Woman pilots her vessel with grace and fortitude through stormy seas. 37

Fifth Discourse: Sleep and counsels of the night 49

Sixth Discourse: A time to sleep vs the morning pillow....63

Seventh Discourse: The Valiant Woman is the "sun" of her household, giving light and warmth. 77

Eighth Discourse: The Valiant Woman considers the "good things" for her children, and is always the first to rise. 91

Ninth Discourse: Developing firmness with constancy, the Valiant Woman is neither obstinate nor fickle. 103

Tenth Discourse: The Valiant Woman has the strength from God to overcome whatever evil with goodness and gentleness of heart. 117

Eleventh Discourse: Goodness enlarges the heart of the Valiant Woman. She has that tranquillity of order which is the essence of peace..129

Twelfth Discourse: The Valiant Woman is magnanimous. She loves the poor, and visits the sick. 139

Thirteenth Discourse: Duties of the Valiant Woman, the guardian of the domestic hearth. 155

Fourteenth Discourse: The virtuous wife can polish the manners of a stern husband, however abrasive his character..167

Fifteenth Discourse: True beauty: a veil of glory that radiates the exterior of the woman who has the invisible elegance of a virtuous heart. 179

Sixteenth Discourse: God has entrusted these children to you and they live in your house. The Valiant Woman knows her children well and cares for every aspect of their lives. Nothing escapes her notice. 191

Seventeenth Discourse: A recapitulation of the sixteen discourses: the fruit of valiance..203

First Discourse
A portrait of the Valiant Woman

Who shall find a valiant woman? Far and from the uttermost coasts is the price of her. The heart of her husband trusteth in her: and he shall have no need of spoils. She will render him good, and not evil, all the days of her life. (Prov. 31:10-12)

All scripture, inspired of God, is profitable to teach, to reprove, to correct, to instruct in justice: That the man of God may be perfect, furnished to every good work. (II Tim. 3:16, 17)

MY CHILDREN,

The Fathers of the Church teach us that the Holy Scriptures are like a vast plain enamelled with lovely flowers, whereon plants — the most varied, the most beautiful, and the most exquisitely tinted — grow and develop themselves to delight our vision, and to prepare sweet cooling fruits for our refreshment in the days of autumn. Nothing in effect is more sublime than the teaching of Holy Writ, nothing more beautiful, more simple, and at the same time more gently persuasive. The words of the Holy Book have a special flavor, a light proper to themselves, a warmth and earnestness which penetrate the heart and subdue it with a sweet, all-powerful emotion. No writing of man has ever wrought the same marvellous results. A single word of the

Bible falling on good ground becomes the seed which gives fruit a hundred-fold, and prepares an abundant harvest of virtue in the soul. See yon tiny seed borne on the breath of the wind. Examine it closely, and you will find it fitted with a delicate yet strong apparatus resembling wings, which enables it to float thus lightly and gracefully in mid-air. It sails on at the sweet will of providence, whose paternal eye is ever watching over it, and when its hour of germination is ripe, it seems as though a gentle guiding hand softly lowered it to some quiet spot of earth, where it sinks into the ground, and in due time bursts forth again out of its bosom, and arises laden with fruits. In like manner do the words of Scripture act in our souls. Thanks to the preaching of the evangelists, the air is full of those divine seeds; the winged germs are floating all round us, and when a heart is ready for their reception, the breath of grace bears to it one of those wondrous grains, which come we know not how, and which may in time bring forth a forest of wide-spreading trees. "And the ground shall bring forth its increase, and the trees shall be filled with fruit."[1]

I have several times had occasion, my children, during these our monthly meetings, to mention for your consideration texts of Scripture bearing on your principal duties, and I rejoice at this opportunity of doing you the justice to say, that the seed has always fallen on good ground, and this is not the least among the consolations enjoyed by your pastor. For a long time past I have wished to comment on an admirable chapter in the book of *Proverbs*, on the *Valiant Woman,* as I seemed to see in it, beforehand, many important counsels for the practical guidance of your lives; because the Scripture, which often alludes to the duties of women, has given therein an epitome of the subject of its teaching. Today, accordingly, I shall commence, and shall continue to preach on all its verses in succession, according as their meaning shall unfold itself to my mind.

[1] Lev. 26:4.

First Discourse

"Who shall find a valiant woman?" The Lord has wrought all His works by two and two, says Holy Writ, and contrast is one of the laws of creation: "So look upon all the works of the Most High two and two, and one against another." This contrast is very striking in the creation of man and woman, and in the distribution of their various qualities; to man is given, in a special manner, strength, wisdom, and mental understanding; to woman, docility, the intelligence of the heart, and that mysterious instinct for a hundred things which escape man's notice. It is true the gifts of one of these wondrous creatures are not entirely denied to the other. I am only pointing out the qualities which, according to the ordinary laws of nature, usually predominate in a mass, in which, however, qualities must continually vary. Thus, although strength of character is not generally considered a prevailing quality in women, it does not thence follow that women are devoid of force and courage, nor that men may not often show themselves the weaker vessels of the two. We are only concerned now with what is habitually the case — with the ordinary character and special gifts usually assigned to women, and with their mission in this world. We must also bear in mind that closely associated with every good quality is to be found the opposite defect, and therefore softness and docility of character may easily degenerate into weakness and inconstancy, owing to the infirmities of our poor human nature. This made Saint Thomas say that the delicacy of a woman's nature is, in a great measure, the cause of the weakness with which she is reproached. And therefore the Wise Man testifies to the experience and the opinion of all ages when he says, "Who shall find a valiant woman?" The answer might be more quickly given if he asked, Who shall find a giddy, frivolous woman, blowing hot and cold alternately? Who shall find that volatile being who passes with lightning rapidity from one opinion to another, as formless as those strange creatures we find decomposing on the sea-shores? Who shall find that nature, variable as the wind, altering her convictions with every fresh change of weather, or caprice of an unreasoning crowd? To such questions the answers would be instant, and the applications numerous. But who shall find a valiant woman? She who can draw from stores of never-failing courage the necessary energy to make head against all the difficulties of her position, its daily worries, hourly anxieties, and ever-recurring contradictions and disappointments. She who can bear up bravely under the many inevitable shocks of life; under family jars, interior depression, and all those slights and wounds which, like the legions of insects in autumn, are perpetually assailing the heart of a woman; she who presides with unvarying prudence over the labors of her household and all the details of housekeeping; who rules her servants wisely, and preserves due order in the arrangement of that multitude of petty affairs which follow on one another through every hour of the day as quickly as the clouds of heaven flit across the sky. Who shall find a valiant woman, who shows herself superior to disaster, to calumny, to the malice of men, and to the many blows of fate; and who, when the violence of the waves is spent, still remains firmly rooted in the sea, a beacon and a light to poor shipwrecked mariners? *Mulierem fortem quis inveniet?*

Later on in the course of our explanation of the verses to come of this chapter, we shall have occasion to return in detail to this important subject; therefore, today I shall confine myself to a few short reflections.

Good understanding, firmness of character, and a combination of natural talent, may in a great measure contribute to the formation of that grand moral nature, which, in its perfection, is entitled by Scripture, "The Valiant Woman;" but what daily excites my admiration for the Fathers of the Church is the marvellous skill with which they cultivated the soil of human nature, assiduously profiting by the least tokens of fertility to sow therein the seed of the Gospel, and enrich it with the grace of Jesus Christ. For religion alone can give to character that firm resolution, grand energy, and steady perseverance which are the crown of our noblest faculties. Without the supernatural aid of

First Discourse

God, human nature is too poor and weak to produce, far less ripen, those fruits of virtue, that exquisite blossom of a heavenly plant, which the Holy Spirit is everywhere seeking under the title of a "valiant woman." *Mulierem fortem quis inveniet?* Be true Christian women, really and sincerely religious; make God the habitual guide and help of your whole lives, and then only will you resemble that ideal of strength and constancy of which Christian heroines have left us so many examples, causing even pagan philosophers to exclaim, "How admirable are these Christian women!"[1] You will become one with God, by the habit of seeking Him in all things, and having recourse to Him as to your first, best friend, alike in joy as in sorrow. This elevating intercourse forms, as it were, an invisible cement, binding together your thoughts, feelings, desires, and resolutions, until the stones of your life, that is, your acts, blend into one solid, united mass, like the buildings of the ancient Romans so often mentioned in history, which have withstood the ravages of time, and remain, even to this day, imperishable monuments, because of that cement, hard as bronze, which rendered them indestructible. Thus have been formed the Christian heroines, who have left such admirable examples to posterity; in this school the virgins and martyrs, the Agneses, the Perpetuas, and the Apollonias learned heroism; and in this same school, also, have many other women, whose energy has been developed in a less dazzling sphere, found strength to bear that daily, life-long, petty martyrdom, in which nature is destroyed and immolated on the altar of duty. Sublime immolation, which caused Saint Ambrose to say, "What a countless number of Christ's martyrs do we find in the obscure paths of daily life!" and Saint Gregory the Great, "If we preserve steadfast patience amidst the ills of life, we shall share in the glory of martyrdom as much as if we had fallen beneath the axe of the executioner." It is there, also, that is nourished and perfected, by divine help, that gentle loving forbearance and wonderful self-devotion, which is daily manifested by virgins consecrated to God, in their

---

[1] Chrys. *ad Vid. Junior*, vol. i, p. 416.

schools, orphanages, hospitals, and visits to the poor. Nothing short of the grace which gave birth to martyrs can produce such hourly prodigies. Ought it then to be difficult, my children, to obtain among Christians an answer to the question, "Who shall find a valiant woman?" Christ's blood has watered the seed and caused it to bring forth fruit. May His grace make it do so a hundred-fold in this our present association. And when men are puzzled to solve those words of Scripture, may they turn to your ranks to find their solution, and ever meet therein many bright examples of the rare virtues of the valiant woman. Was it not to a Christian woman Saint Chrysostom addressed this magnificent eulogy? — "You possess a science which rises superior to storms; you have that energy of a strong mind which is more powerful than many armies, more safe than walls and fortified towers." We cannot believe that this race of noble women is extinct among the Christians of this day.

The Holy Scripture continues — "Far and from the uttermost coasts is the price of her." Saint Gregory Nazianzen tells us, "There is nothing better than a good woman; nothing worse than a bad one." A good woman is the most precious of the treasures of her house; she is its life and light, shedding brilliant rays around her, multiplied by countless reflections; she is its soul, pervading everything, and leaving everywhere traces of her gentle influence. The Holy Ghost, treating of this same subject, does not hesitate to make use of a simile generally reserved to express the beneficent action of the Deity — "As the sun when it riseth to the world in the high places of God, so is the beauty of a good wife for the ornament of her house."[1] Then, as if fearing enough had not been said, the Holy Spirit adds to, and heightens its praise, by comparing the countenance of such a woman to the brightness of the lights in the golden candlesticks in the Temple of Jerusalem — "As the lamp shining upon the holy candlestick, so is the beauty of the face in a ripe age."[2] You see, my children, that if the Bible contains some severe strictures

[1] Ecclus. 26:21.
[2] Ecclus. 26:22.

on women, it repays them with usury by the praises it lavishes on such among them as by their virtues and eminent qualities have made themselves the glory of their sex. As the feminine nature is usually inclined to extremes, do you try to be of the number of those women whose price is above rubies and pearls brought from afar. Let not the other two sentences of Holy Writ, "A man will choose any wickedness but the wickedness of a woman," and "All malice is short to the malice of a woman,"[1] be ever in any point applicable to you.

"The heart of her husband trusteth in her and he hath no need of spoils." Mutual confidence, my children, is the very breath of life, the source of the purest happiness; it binds hearts closer, and weaves fresh charms for the ties of relationship. Where trust does not exist there can only be a life more appalling than the grave; that is, one devoid of its proper elements, and whose respiration is continually oppressed and troubled. Were I preaching to your husbands, I would say to them, "Seek to deserve the entire confidence of your wives, for heartfelt, loving trust can neither be compelled nor given at will; it must be won by virtue." This perfect trust takes rank among such elevated matters, that God has not placed it at the free disposition or pleasure of man, and for this we should render Him thanks, for in no other way could He have so triumphantly protected the grandest attribute of humanity, — admiration for all that is good and noble. I would therefore say to your husbands, "Have you not yourselves only to accuse if you have lost the respect and confidence of your wives?" But it is not to them I speak; it is to you, ladies, whom it is my ardent wish to see good, worthy, admirable women, whatever may be the difficulties of your position. Exert yourselves to merit and win your husbands' confidence, which you will infallibly do, if you lead an exemplary life, and maintain unshaken sweetness and patience amidst what may be most wounding to you. A man may have great defects, even great vices; he may have his irritable moments, when he will use words as harsh as they are

[1] Ecclus. 25:19, 26.

unjust towards her who is the helpmate of his life. That is of little matter. If a woman is all she should be, he will respect her in spite of himself, and place full trust in her; and notwithstanding the angry taunts, in the truth of which a passionate man professes to believe at the moment of utterance, his heart will remain faithful to her, and will be likewise drawn to admire and practice virtue, one of its exclusive prerogatives being that man cannot long persevere in contemning it when he sees it firm and unchanged amid the severest trials.

But how happy is the household where the hearts of husband and wife are drawn together by mutual trust, where the two become fused in one, and each leans naturally on the other, like two vases of which the first contains a liquid necessary to the second. Such a union is one of the most precious blessings heaven can bestow; it is the crown and happiness of life, says one of the Fathers of the Church; a paradise on earth, and, next to the joys of heaven and those which faith can give even in this land of exile it is the purest foretaste of that better life, where we shall at length fully enjoy all that the heart desires and longs for — regard, trust, and pure love, through all eternity. In this life of perfect union, the husband infuses into his wife's mind a share of his intelligence, good sense, prudence, and resolution; while, on her side, the wife beautifies and adorns her husband's life. Like a lovely tree, she bears for him the refreshing fruits of a loving heart. She dries his tears; she compensates him for all his toils and labors; she pours into his veins the oil of peace and happiness. "A virtuous woman," saith the Holy Spirit, "rejoiceth her husband: and shall fulfil the years of his life in peace. . . . The grace of a diligent woman shall delight her husband, and shall fat his bones."[1]

Happy indeed the man who possesses such a companion! "He hath no need of spoils." He finds his heart's best treasure in his own home, and foreign attractions possess no charms for him. The beauty, the virtues, and the love of his wife are the chains forged by providence to bind him to the path of duty.

[1] Ecclus. 26:2, 16.

First Discourse

Taking this verse in yet another sense, we may also say that the husband hath no need of spoils, because his wife, as we shall explain more fully later, by her care, attention, foresight, and economy, is a source of ever-increasing wealth to his house; therefore he is not compelled to have recourse to those dubious ways of money-making, among which usury, fraudulent gains, and the gambling spirit of the stock exchange are conspicuous.

"The valiant woman will render her husband good, and not evil, all the days of her life." What a noble quality providence hereby accords to women! To render good always, evil never. To render good always, above all to her husband, for she should form but one being with him; to render good under all circumstances and in every way, by words, deeds, counsels, even by silence. To render good, by foreseeing the perplexities and annoyances which must attend her husband's path in life, and laboring to remove them. To render good, when he is in health and prosperity, by rejoicing in his joy and sharing in his happiness; but yet more, to render him good in his hours of pain and sorrow, by seeking to soothe and alleviate his sufferings, by the many tender, delicate attentions which woman is so skilful in discovering how to pay where she loves. She will render good always, evil never! Evil never! Remember, I insist on that point; for a woman has so many ways of rendering evil if she wishes, so many resources to aid her vengeance, and enable her to scatter thorns around her, when her heart has been lacerated. I beseech you, my children, in the name of God and of your own dearest interests — in the name of your family and of your sex — never have recourse to such expedients, even though your husband should be passionate, selfish, and vindictive, and have been guilty of wounding your feelings in the most sensitive part. Stay; I am wrong. There is a noble revenge open to you — to render him good! Oppose an act of abnegation, of self-denial, to each act of selfishness; speak a gentle word for every harsh one. Or, if you cannot do that, at least keep silence; not an aggressive, provoking silence, but one born of love and patience; and next day, or even that evening, perfect your work of vengeance by redoubling every mark of tenderness and attention. Ah! if you would only learn to revenge yourselves in this manner, what victories you would win! What magnanimous contests! What entire and peaceful triumphs! It was thus Saint Monica prevailed over a husband of violent temper, and prone to those disorders which are most wounding to a wife's feelings. She avoided all irritating discussions with him; she waited for the day of divine mercy. To his passionate outbreaks she only opposed calmness and silence; and whenever she judged it necessary to justify to him her own conduct, she waited until he was appeased and master of himself. It was this behavior, continues Saint Augustine, which gained her the respectful love and admiration of her husband, and led to the conversion of him with whom she had so patiently borne. To all the women who confided to her ear complaints of their home life, she answered by laying the blame on their own tongues, and counselling them in a tone of pleasant raillery. And when these women, knowing the violent temper of Saint Augustine's father, were amazed that none had ever heard of his beating his wife, or of the good understanding between them being interrupted for even a single day, and sought to learn Saint Monica's secret, she taught them her mode of conduct. Those who followed it had cause to congratulate themselves; those who took no heed of it, continued to live in a painful thraldom. Even her mother-in-law had allowed herself to be prejudiced against her by perfidious insinuations, but disarmed at last by Saint Monica's untiring patience and demeanor, full of sweetness and respect, she came of her own accord and denounced to her son the envenomed tongues which were disturbing the peace of his household; and from thenceforth they all lived together in affectionate union. Do you, my children, imitate so beautiful an example; that will be the best answer to many objections, the surest means of avoiding many snares, and of causing to disappear a great portion of the obstacles which oppose themselves to concord in families. Imitate this holy soul, of whom

First Discourse

Saint Augustine says also, that she never interfered in quarrels or animosities save to pacify; and, though often made a confidant of embittered and angry feelings, she never repeated to the persons interested any speeches which would not tend to reconcile them with each other.

We will finish this discourse by the concluding words of the verse. "She will render him good, and not evil, all the days of her life." Yes, all the days of her life! While a husband is still young and strong, and retaining traces of his early attractions, it is perhaps easy to render him good. But later on appear the wrinkles of old age, and maladies with all their painful attendants come to knock at his door, while his temper too frequently becomes gloomy, morose, unmanageable, and irritable by reason of his failing powers. Then is the hour of trial of true affection, for then is needed redoubled care, attention, kind services, and self-devotion. The juice of the grape is called the milk of old men, and the saying is still truer of the wine of affection. You should have in your heart some drops of that old wine; you will have an abundance of it, if you have retained some from youth and middle age. Give each day a cup filled to the brim with it to your husband, whose strength already fails, and whose brow bears traces of the end of his autumn, and the commencement of his winter. "Give wine to them that are grieved in mind,"[1] says the Holy Spirit. And the best of all wine, that which best renews the life-blood of the heart, which would perhaps become frozen by the cold breath of indifference, is the wine of affection.

Religion alone can make women truly valiant in all the circumstances of life; it alone can render them superior to all the accidents and misfortunes of existence, the repugnances of nature, the defects of character, and the continual annoyances and wounds by which the heart is, as it were, ground between heavy stones, or, what is not less painful, lacerated by a thousand needle-points.

[1] Prov. 31:6.

Real sincere piety can alone develop in women that moral strength which overcomes difficulties, making them like birds which soar above the clouds and tempests, and enabling them to fulfil all their duties with the serenity of heavenly peace. But to carry out the resemblance to birds, there must be wings, and God alone can adorn the soul with those celestial wings, strong yet light, with which she mounts swiftly aloft, as if disputing the prize of force and agility with the princes of the air, according to the comparison of the Prophet, "That take their diversion with the birds of the air."[1]

Our power often lies in making use of those wings of the soul, especially when they are animated by the spirit of wisdom. May then our Lord bestow them on you as on the woman of whom the Scripture speaks; they will not be superfluous in assisting you to fulfil your mission of valiant women. *Datæ sunt mulieri alae duae.*[2]

---

[1] Bar. 3:17.
[2] Apoc. 12:14.

Second Discourse
The Valiant Woman reigns over one empire, and that is her home.

She hath sought wool and flax, and hath wrought by the counsel of her hands. (Prov. 31:13)

MY CHILDREN,

In our last discourse we commenced by sketching the portrait of the valiant woman, as traced by the Holy Spirit in the book of Proverbs. The valiant woman, of mild yet energetic character, comprehending and fulfilling her duties with steadfast perseverance; the valiant woman, rising superior to the miseries of this world, the malice of men, and the injustice of opinion; who, presiding with graceful dignity over all the details of her household, is like unto the sun lighting up and vivifying the universe. The valiant woman is a rare being — as rare and precious as the pearls which come from afar. Is this rarity caused by woman's delicate nature exercising so great an influence over her character that it communicates to her ideas, projects, and resolutions, a want of constancy and energy? Sts. Thomas and Albert the Great do not scruple to assert that it is so. Or is it caused by over-indulgence in her education, effeminate habits, and the absence of those fixed religious principles which color the whole life? I think all these causes may contribute towards it; and I will add, taking it only in a good point of view, that our Creator dispenses His gifts unequally to the works of His hands: thus beside a person in whom a certain quality predominates we find another in whom it does not exist, or only in a lesser degree. The two following verses furnish us with a very exact epitome of a wife's duties towards her husband. She should merit his confidence by her virtues and good qualities; and her life should be devoted to cheering and adorning that of her husband by her unvarying amiability.

The Wise Man continues — The valiant woman "hath sought wool and flax, and hath wrought by the counsel of her hands." This verse brings us to speak of woman's occupations, and, in order to leave nothing unsaid, we will discourse today on manual works, and in our next conference on intellectual labors.

The care of her household should be one of a woman's chief occupations. To men belong external toil, the hurry of business, the administration of civil and military offices, the courts of law, the cure of the sick, and the study of science. Woman plays a more modest part: her domain is her house, her rule is over its interior, her subjects are the persons and things connected with all the details of domestic life. Woman's mission as well as man's has its advantages and inconveniences. Flowers and thorns are to be found in all the gardens of earth, whether these belong to man or woman, and happiness often depends on the degree of skill and care with which we cull the flowers and put aside the thorns.

There are some characters who possess the unhappy talent of never seeing a thorn without coming in contact with it in some awkward manner; pricks never fail them so much the more surely, that even where thorns do not exist, they manage to implant those of their own nature, which are neither the least numerous nor the least sharp.

Accept then, my children, the position God has ordained for you in this world; accept the sphere in which Divine Providence has placed you; be queens in your own empire; but if you value your happiness, your tranquillity, and the success of your affairs, do not seek to be queens elsewhere. If prudence permit and wisdom counsel, then suggest, advise, and influence by affection; but you will be all the more persuasive if you are first what you ought yourselves to be, and what God has intended you should be. To do good in one's own sphere of action, without seeking to leave it unless when requested to do so, is often the best sermon, and the most active means of indirectly influencing affairs outside our own province.

Saint Gregory Nazianzen says, in writing of his mother, that she practiced perfectly the advice contained in the book of Proverbs, devoting herself so successfully to domestic affairs, that one might have thought she had no leisure for those of Heaven; and yet so truly pious, as to appear a stranger to all household questions. Neither of these obligations interfered with the other, but they seemed reciprocally to strengthen and perfect each other.

These words, my children, are the evident confirmation of many truths but little known, which I have frequently endeavored to explain to you in my discourses. Piety, when true, injures nothing; on the contrary, it tends to perfect all, even the care of our temporal affairs. It doubles the powers of heart and mind, it infuses marvellous activity; and the time given to God, far from taking aught from our temporal concerns, enlivens our attention to them and insures their success. Piety and religious duties may be likened to the food and drink which are given to the reaper during his labors under the summer's sun; it is evident in a mathematical point of view, that he must lose a little time in eating his dinner, drinking, and taking a few moments' rest. Yet who would call that wasted time? It is the same thing with true piety: if it be well understood, and if it be enlightened, it can never be injurious to the care of a household or the attention due to domestic affairs. I wish, my children, that each of you may merit the praises bestowed by Saint Gregory on his mother; for if every woman practiced piety like her, such a daughter of Heaven would be less ill-spoken of by worldlings. I desire that every one may be able to say of each of you, "That woman has found the secret of working so well and successfully in the interests of her family, that she appears to reserve no time for God and spiritual matters, yet she is so pious that her life seems detached from all external things." I acknowledge this holy combination is difficult to carry out; but why not try to accomplish it since it is so good, so useful to your own interests, and so beneficial to the interests of religion?

After these preliminary considerations, we will return to the explanation of our verse. "She hath sought wool and flax, and hath wrought by the counsel of her hands." And further on, the Scripture adds, "Her fingers have taken hold of the spindle." One of the greatest misfortunes of many women is not knowing how to occupy themselves — that is, occupy themselves in manual labor, not that I mean to exclude intellectual work, of which I intend to speak later. One cannot with impunity infringe the laws of Providence; and though there may be some exceptional cases, the general rule does not the less hold good. God has given you the care of household matters and the ordering of domestic affairs, even in their smallest details. You possess a certain amount of activity allotted to you by Providence for that purpose; if you do not so employ it, it may turn to your injury by being changed into something noxious or vicious. What is more common in our day than the sentimental woman who fancies herself misunderstood? I do not wish to speak too harshly of those sickly imaginations, which deserve as much pity as blame, but do they not themselves tend to make their evil incurable? And if their minds are not comprehended, is it not because their mode of life is rather incomprehensible? In place of occupying themselves with things suitable to their sex, they pass their time in dreaming. Their brain is always busy with some fantastic project; they are perpetually building castles in the air, while practical women prefer the domain of realities, so that when they meet they cannot understand each other. Nothing is more likely to develop spleen than this chimerical state of

Second Discourse

existence; the nerves, being constantly on the stretch, grow weakened, irritated, and sickly, the malady becomes chronic, and the whole being out of tune, until such persons are very like to those sensitive plants which shrink from the lightest touch, yet whose principal cause of irritation, though unsuspected by themselves, is from within. I remember meeting formerly in the mountains of Narvan, women who inhabited the most wretched huts; up at sunrise every morning, and possessing blooming countenances and vigorous health, I can assure you these women never suffered from *ennui* and spleen — they had no time for that.

If you wish, my children, to be strong in mind and body, avoid with the utmost care that dreamland, those aerial journeys, in which both heart and intelligence are wasted on nothing. If you have no other occupation, I would rather you should walk on the Mall; [1] at all events, the sea air does good and expands the chest, whilst the atmosphere of some reveries causes physical and moral disease, especially if to them be added the perusal of novels, more or less sensual, which produce the same effect on the soul that opium and other Eastern narcotics do on the body — effeminate, melancholy, perhaps voluptuous reveries. Idle dreaming and romances! you have destroyed more women than sickness has ever done! Occupation being one of the principal remedies for this most serious evil, I shall first speak of external employments and manual labors. Listen to Saint Clement of Alexandria: "Bodily labor is suitable for women; . . . all kinds of needlework and embroidery; all the different cares which the welfare of their family, of whom they are the natural and prescribed guardians, require of them. . . . Their duty is to watch and anticipate their husband's wishes and wants; . . . to keep the clothing necessary for their family in good order; to prepare with their own hands, if needful, food and drink, and place them before their husbands with all the grace of loving amiability. . . . By acting thus, the health of the body is strengthened, and our

---

[1] The Mall is a walk at La Rochelle, on the sea-shore.

The Valiant Woman

Lord loves women of this type. He loves to see them always occupied in useful labors, holding in their hands the distaff or the needle, . . . and not omitting to follow Sarah's example in dispensing to wearied travellers all the attentions dictated by benevolent hospitality."

My children, the most distinguished women of ancient times, even queens and princesses, devoted their leisure hours to needlework and the spinning wheel, and disdained none of those labors which in the present day many look on almost as a disgrace. The Latin historian recounts that Alexander the Great, after taking prisoner the mother of Darius and some members of the royal family, sent them garments made in Macedon, with the people who had worked them, in order that the royal family might take patterns and make similar ones. The queen-mother burst into tears, regarding this proceeding as an insult; for the Persians, an effeminate and corrupt nation, looked on such work as unworthy of noble ladies. Alexander hearing of this, thought himself bound to offer an apology. "I erred," he said, "in treating you according to Grecian customs; for this robe you see me wear is not only a gift from my sisters, but also the work of their own hands." Plutarch relates in his *Life of Augustus*, that this Roman emperor seldom wore any vesture but what was made by his wife, his daughter, or some other member of his family. We must confess our customs are far removed from those of the ancients. Are we the better for it? Is our health more vigorous, our imagination calmer? Are our habits more genuine, more in accordance with a wholesome nature? We may well doubt it. Do you wish to hear Christian authorities on the same subject? They are not wanting. Saint Jerome recommends to women the weaving of wool, the spinning of thread, and every occupation of that nature; he does not hesitate to call things by their right names, and speaks of the spindle, the wool, the distaff, and the wheel, not omitting the hand which so skillfully manipulates all committed to it. Charlemagne made his daughters learn all sorts of needlework, and on being asked the reason replied, "In the first place, to make them avoid idleness; and secondly, as no one possesses a guarantee against the blows of fate, should any adverse fortune befall them, they will be enabled to provide for their own necessities." Charlemagne's reasons are grave and solid; be good enough to devote a few moments to their consideration.

First, it is essential for a woman to avoid idleness. It is the mother of all vice. An idle woman feels the need of continually going abroad to supply her want of employment in her own house; did she not take this — for her, unfortunately, necessary — precaution she would die of *ennui* at home. But when she goes out she talks, she wounds charity, she makes enemies, she divulges family secrets, she commits a multitude of imprudences in words and actions, and when she returns home, feels worse than before. It is idleness which draws a woman from her domestic duties, and by creating in her a craving for excitement, introduces the most deplorable disorder and negligence into her household. Everything is left to servants — children and business alike; every one deteriorates physically and morally; her husband is discontented, and the family hearth, which should be a nest full of love and repose, is made unbearable to all. Bad thoughts also take birth easily in an unoccupied mind; this dangerous seed quickly spreads, and multiplies like weeds in a neglected garden. The time comes when such a woman falls; one knows not how it happened, she perhaps cannot tell herself; the fall has been as sudden as a slip on the ice. The first and principal cause was idleness, which insensibly, under the name of recreation, conducted her on the verdant turf; that turf in many places covered the brink of precipices; a single step was enough; once on the slope, she slipped, and then nothing could save her.

Another serious evil which springs from idleness is *ennui*. It spreads like a funeral pall over the whole of life. Work, though laborious, gives happiness. It completes our existence, and makes it fruitful; we feel that we live, and we are happy in the fullness of vital strength. But the life of an idle man is a blank; his faculties become enervated, then diseased, and when thus diseased, cause torture to the soul which they are slowly poisoning. A very rich man, whom I once knew, spent part of his day exclaiming, "How bored I feel; I am rich, yet, I weary of everything." He would have been far happier with poverty for his inheritance, and labor for his wealth. The chief cause of his weariness was that he led an idle, unoccupied life, perpetually reverting to itself like the branches of the weeping willow.

The second reason given by Charlemagne sounds strange from the mouth of an illustrious emperor. He was afraid that his daughters might some day be reduced to poverty, and desired that they should be able to support themselves in such a case. That crowned heads, in our days, should hold such language, can easily be understood; but that Charlemagne, at the head of a vast empire, in which revolutionary ideas were unknown, should express a like fear, may well appear at first sight a little extraordinary. But this great prince had the keen, clear insight of genius; like all superior men who are raised to a height above others, he felt more deeply the emptiness in human things, and little confidence in the stability of aught that is mortal. Be that as it may, his advice is most useful for the present generation. We live in an epoch of such agitation that people, from one cause or another, may quickly become embarrassed, and it is but prudent to have more than one string to one's bow. How many families have I known who have had reason to bless Providence for having given them a taste for work, even in their days of affluence. The hour of misfortune has come, yet the entire family has derived a competence from the exercise of talents acquired and perfected in earlier days. No one could have better grounds for feeling security in the future than Charlemagne had, yet that powerful emperor was not without anxiety for what might befall his children. Do not you either be neglectful; without becoming a pessimist, do not give way to a blind confidence, make yourself and your children look on work as something holy, or at least very serviceable, and infuse into all around you a love of constant and useful occupation.

Second Discourse

There is one objection which I wish to answer, and I shall find therein an occasion for a salutary spiritual counsel. It has been remarked that manual labor, needlework particularly, possessed one great drawback for women; their brain being more active than their fingers, for every stitch made by the needle, the lively imagination traverses leagues, and often in arid, unwholesome regions, or through stifling atmospheres. The brain becomes excited, the nerves overwrought, and then manual labor is doubly fatiguing.[1] Formerly, when piety reigned supreme in their minds, and their faculties were held in equilibrium by a tranquil faith, work had not this danger for women, or at least not in the same high degree; there were always verdant spots whereon the expanding mind could repose; the needle brought fatigue but to the hand, and that only at the end of its prolonged use.

But now, when imaginations are excited by the numberless productions of working brains, and often by the reading of those books in which one might say the author had dropped grains of gunpowder, which only wait their hour of explosion in inflammable minds — now when, in some souls, nothing is firmly established; neither ideas, nor feelings, nor convictions, I can well understand that a purely manual occupation may fatigue and bring about dangerous reactions in a brain already too highly wrought. I see but one remedy for this grave evil, and I would say to all women: Be true Christians; then your heads and your hearts will not be in a constant state of effervescence; your thoughts and affections will rest in the calm of a tranquil conscience, and you may feel sure that needlework will no longer be the cause of a moral dizziness, nor of those feverish ideas which are the torment of our age. Imitate even our ancestors. If propriety and the place permit

---

[1] "I have been stitching a sheet and have sewed many things besides into my work. ... A misty, dark, melancholy day within and without. I felt more depressed than usual, but as I did not wish to yield to *ennui*, I took up my sewing to kill it at the point of the needle; but the wicked serpent still lives, though I have cut off his head and his tail, that is, indolence and dreamy thoughts." -*Journal of Eugenie de Guérin* pp. 123-147.

it, sing while you work, and shun not the joyous canticles and simple expressions of a happy soul. Song seems to have wings to bear sadness away; it brings all into harmony, even unstrung minds.

In order to leave nothing unfinished, I will treat in my next discourse of the intellectual labors proper for a woman; and now I will conclude by a short *résumé* of our reflections. Employ yourselves actively in the interior arrangements of your household; obviously you cannot do everything, but you can do some things; and even where you do not personally act, you should still direct and overlook. Do not disdain to inspect your house at times from the attic to the cellar: a mistress's eye is everywhere needful. Let your servants understand that you are thoroughly acquainted with your own house, that no corner in it is unknown, no recess hidden from your eyes; that you could instantly detect an object wanting in any spot, and that you are even competent to give them practical lessons in their various duties. Nothing keeps servants so much on the alert as this conviction. I presume, of course, all this is done without fuss and scoldings, wisely and kindly. You will also observe, that where the eye and active mind of the mistress of a house are duly exercised, there is always to be found a readiness, a zeal, and a cheerful alacrity which no other means can ever produce. It is because the valiant woman, according to the beautiful imagery of the Holy Book, is truly a sun in the interior of her house.[1] Suppose for an instant that the sun should suddenly disappear; all objects in nature will remain as they were, but before long everything fades, shrivels up, and dies; but let the star of day return to the horizon and at once everything gains new life, becomes vivified, animated, and fully developed.

So acts a good, energetic woman. She is the sun rising above the hills, and her blooming, joyous countenance sheds a radiance over all her household.

---

[1] "As the sun when it riseth to the world in the high places of God, so is the beauty of a good wife for the ornament of her house." — Ecclus.26:21.

Third Discourse
Prudence in balancing the domestic economy with other healthy pursuits...

Such is a wise and silent woman: and there is nothing so much worth as a well instructed soul. (Ecclus. 26:18)

MY CHILDREN,

It seems to me that I shall not be deviating from our program, if I borrow my text of today from another book of Holy Writ, which completes the description given in that of Proverbs of the valiant woman; so much the more that the inspiration of all the sacred writings being derived from the same source, it may be truly said that it is always the same Author who is quoted.

One of a woman's chief duties is the care of her family and the government of her household, and of everything relating to its domestic economy. Saint Gregory Nazianzen's mother is an admirable model in this respect. For this holy doctor tells us that she practiced to perfection the counsels contained in the book of Proverbs, devoting herself with such success to her domestic affairs as to seem to have no leisure for attending to heavenly matters, and yet so absorbed in religion, that one might have believed all household questions were foreign to her thoughts. These two obligations need never clash, but may, on the contrary, reciprocally strengthen and perfect each other.

In our last discourse we dwelt particularly on the necessity of work both with the needle and in the details of housekeeping, and on the activity a woman should exert in her home, in order to watch over and keep all in good order, and we explained the great advantages of these different occupations in promoting virtue and health, and in forming a safeguard against *ennui*, and also in often preventing embarrassments in many affairs.

I do not shut my eyes to the objections which may be raised to my views, such as: Would you then degrade woman to a mere household drudge, and condemn her to superintend nothing higher than cooking? Are you not forgetting that a woman possesses much that is grand and noble in both mind and heart? Are you not treading under foot all the germs of intellect which exist in a woman's brain, and which, after all, though different in kind, may yet fully equal those of which men are so proud and tenacious?

Everywhere in this world, my children, we meet with the Straits of Messina. Pardon me this little geographical detail; it best explains my meaning. Between Calabria and Sicily there exists a strait, three leagues in width, through which two seas send strong currents in opposite directions, thus requiring much skill and experience on the pilot's part to keep his boat in the center. These Straits of Messina aptly illustrate many of the questions which present themselves in this life. On either side of us are strong currents or exaggerations. It is not always easy to keep in the middle, and the more so as from both sides one is assailed by red-hot bullets; that is to say, by angry outbursts or more or less violent contradictions. For example, in the question now occupying us, if women are recommended to devote themselves seriously to household affairs, the partisans of their intellectual and moral emancipation rush forward, armed at all points, exclaiming — "What! you would then debase women to stupid simpletons." On the other hand, there may be excess in the quantity of intellectual food, in the application to it, in the studies chosen, in their practical

Third Discourse

results; for, as Fénelon has well said, "All is lost if a woman neglects her domestic cares in order to shine as a wit and a blue-stocking;"[1] and she is the more exposed to danger, "... because (you will pardon the Archbishop of Cambray this opinion) women run a risk of going into extremes in everything."[2] The middle line is the line of wisdom, said the ancients, and it is this middle line which I wish to recommend you in this instruction.

Can and ought a woman occupy her time with study, reading, poetry, literature, fine arts, and music? To a question put in such a general manner, it would be very difficult to give an answer, for it is evident that there must be many women who could not take up these branches of learning — some from want of leisure, others from want of the necessary capacity good sense demands; therefore, that we should first eliminate a certain category of women, and their number must be determined by reason rather than by abstract theories. But what are we to say to those who have leisure, and more or less capacity? Before entering on the narrow, dangerous path of a distinct, decided reply, it would be well to name three essential conditions, which should always be the accompaniments of study in woman's life. Household duties must never be neglected, nor the due ordering of family affairs, for study must not interfere with more important duties; and should it ever become an obstacle in their way, it is to be condemned, not in itself, but in its excess. If Providence has decreed you more liberty; if, for example, you are not married, or have no children, or are a widow, or have not a very numerous household to superintend, give a little more time to intellectual culture by all means, provided you observe a second condition, that of consulting the measure of your understanding, and not exceeding the amount suited to it. Each mind has its own peculiar strength and quality, as every vase has its size and powers of resistance. You would not try

[1] *Avis à une Dame sur l'Education.*
[2] *Education des Filles*, ch. 11.

to pour the contents of a bottle into a liqueur-glass, nor make waves of heated vapor flow through a slight and fragile tube. Have regard in like manner to the strength of your mind; it was the advice of Horace: "Try," said he, "and see how much your shoulders can bear." If you can only bear one drop, take no more; science, like wine, flies to the head, intoxicates, and makes us dizzy. Unfortunately, pride blinds many on this point, men as much as women; and very often the more foolish and narrow-minded people are, the more clever they imagine themselves to be, like those weak heads who think their brains can stand any amount of insidious liquor. Pay great attention, then, to this condition, for it is a most essential one; your good sense, perhaps your virtue, is concerned in it; for if once the head be turned, it is not easy to say what the heart may do. The right quantity in everything! Vice itself is often merely an infraction of this great rule. The right quantity! — that is true wisdom in the combination of both moral and physical elements and were it only observed, we should everywhere see order replacing disorder, and the prodigy described by the poet renewed —

Aux accords d'Amphion les pierres se mouvaient,
Et sur les murs de Thèbes en ordre se rangeaient.

The third condition which appears to my mind indispensable is that modest reserve which Fénelon characterized as "modesty in knowledge."[1] This modesty will suggest to you the topics which you would do well to ignore; it will teach you to avoid that affected tone, those sententious manners and studied effects, which have perhaps most of all contributed to depreciate the value of study in the life of a woman. Everything in you, even knowledge ought to be simple, gracious, docile, full of sweetness and modesty. These three conditions of time, quantity, and discretion being laid down for the regulating of studies, we shall be more at liberty now to

[1] *Education des Filles*, ch. 7.

Third Discourse

speak of the right teaching; for you will not forget that these three conditions are presupposed in the advice given.

Is it right and suitable for a woman to occupy herself with serious, intellectual questions, not having any bearing on her family duties?

M. de Tocqueville, in his *Correspondence*, draws a charming sketch of character, which I would recommend to the perusal of all who are inimical to the study and intellectual development of women. "Our good friend . . . asks my opinion of Miss ———. Here is what I think and know of her. She is the daughter of an intellectual egotist, and of a narrow-minded, rather silly devotee. . . . This young girl may be sixteen or seventeen at most. Physically, she is a charming creature, but I think her utterly mindless and very commonplace. She is good, gentle, retiring, and narrow-minded; at least, such is her portrait as it has remained in my memory. I do not think there is more in her at present than the promise of a strictly proper woman, and I know no one who gives fewer indications of great qualities. She is, as I said before, very pretty, very much taken up with her toilet, even in the dull, quiet life she leads; and has excelled from childhood in making the most of any scraps of finery for her own and her sisters' adornment. I never heard any other talent attributed to her; and this, joined to the narrowness of her understanding, threatens to render her a very insignificant being, though pretty. . . . The commonplace is the very atmosphere of that house. . . . The virtues of good citizens enveloped in fearfully narrow-minded ideas."[1]

This little sketch is addressed to those who wish to see all women reduced to the level of commonplace, and would almost raise stupidity and ignorance to the rank of virtues. But you, my children, must never look on the character described by M. de Tocqueville as a fit model for Christian women. The God whom we adore is the God of knowledge, and though the ignorant may enter into the Kingdom of Heaven, yet such is not the rule.

[1] *Correspondence*, 1. ii. pp. 345-347.

On the other side, we find a different rock to be avoided, — that pointed out by Madame de Maintenon, who says, perhaps with a little exaggeration, "Women never know anything thoroughly, so the little they do know usually makes them proud, disdainful, talkative, and averse to everything serious."[1] Therefore, the Latin poet asked for a little hearth, a simple roof devoid of smoke, a spring of sparkling water, the herbs of the field, and a wife not over-learned — *non doctissima conjux*.[2] Fénelon dreaded, above all, women too learned in theology; for while he highly commended a real, solid knowledge of religion, he distrusted the doctoral temerity in vogue at that period. "I would much prefer," he says, "that she would be well versed in the housekeeping accounts, than in the disputes of theologians on grace."[3]

To me it seems easy to avoid these excesses. When a woman has fulfilled all her other duties, she may very well occupy herself with elementary science; with literature, with philosophy even, and aim at perfecting herself in these points, which are so full of charms and knowledge. There are different regions in science; and though one does not always reach the summit, one may still ascend the mountain a little way to enjoy the beautiful view; and there is nothing more beautiful than philosophy, especially Christian philosophy, when suitably presented to the mind. Is your heart sad? After prayer, I know no more efficacious remedy than some hours' perusal of an author whose noble ideas and sublime style transport us into those calm, serene regions where men and human affairs are quickly forgotten. Oftentimes, when the moral atmosphere around us seems to grow too stifling, we dream of peace, and say, "Oh! if I could but take refuge on some high mountain to rest, and be alone with God — the sunshine, and beautiful nature — what a happiness it would be! What renewed life! What joy for soul and body!" Why call it a dream? We can

---

[1] *Entretiens sur l'Education*, ent. 8, p. 22.
[2] *Martial*, Epig. 1. ii. p. 90.
[3] *Avis à une Dame sur l'Education*.

give ourselves this pleasure without leaving our own room. Reading and meditation will furnish us with wings; the mind frees itself from matter, it mounts, it flies, it soars aloft to those intellectual mountains on whose heights we shall find peace and serenity. Study has great advantages; it elevates the mind, it enables women through its hidden influence to lead a life of higher aims than the cares of the toilet, as M. de Tocqueville says, and aids them to divest themselves of that petty personality which wraps itself up in a host of trifles and trivial ideas. The mind becomes enlarged by the contact of new thoughts; the study of literature polishes it, and gives it a more agreeable tone, by infusing into it at the same time delicacy and energy; poetry inflames and kindles it with the breath of God-like inspiration; and beautiful music restores its calm, and bestows on it the exquisite sense of harmony in all things. The study of the fine arts develops in it the feeling of the beautiful, and opens to thought horizons hitherto unknown. Let us suppose a noble mind, a superior understanding, with the organization of a woman; let her education be constructed on these principles; let the Graces and Muses combine to form her mind and develop her intelligence in a sweet harmony of powers; let virtue and prudence be always the guardians of her home; and then I will venture to present that noble creature as the ideal Christian woman I like to dream of — an ideal it would be well to seek to imitate, even at a distance. A woman so formed is the chief ornament of her house; she knows how to consult with her cook, and arrange with her all the details of a good dinner; but when she returns to her drawing-room, she knows still better how to carry on an entertaining conversation, not wasting her intellect on matters of dress, but reserving at least a portion of it for serious and instructive discourse, interspersed with observations replete with thought and delicacy. I would not even exclude Latin from this scheme of a perfect education, and if any one reproaches me with too much concession to learned women, I shall invoke two authorities to whom none can cavil — Fénelon and Madame de Swetchine, — and proceed to quote from the latter as follows — "Your Latin," she writes to a friend, "has given me at least as much pleasure as the rest. The language of our faith should never be omitted in any religious education, nor in that which one gives one's self at your age, when one can still learn whatever one wishes. It is not knowledge which makes a pedant, and I can assure you women become such from following a very different plan to that you are pursuing."[1]

A woman of this stamp will never bore her husband; and amongst a woman's good qualities, I would by no means place in the lowest rank that of not boring her husband. Now, of all the sources of *ennui*, especially to a man who is not over patient, I know of none more certain, more unfailing, as M. de Tocqueville says, than a narrow-minded, foolish devotee. Silliness, particularly if one has the unhappy talent of joining it to an ill-understood piety, is capable of spoiling everything, even all that is best. I must strongly insist on this point, my children, for it is most essential with regard to the peace of your families and the morality of your husbands. Physical qualities, if alone, exert a merely temporary and very fleeting influence; but next to virtue, I know nothing more likely to retain the respect and love of a husband than a delicate, well-cultivated mind, which looks on all things from the highest, the most amiable, and most holy point of view. To accomplish this, it is not at all necessary to be a genius; you cannot think with what facility this manner of looking at things becomes naturally, instinctively developed in natures where virtue and a good education have been combined. It is a land where you have deposited that earth which gardeners prize so highly, called peat, and in which the rarest flowers seem to grow spontaneously. The number of women who have alienated the hearts of their husbands, and thus conduced later to

---

[1] Lettres, t. ii. p. 474. Fénelon, in his *Education des Filles*, ch. 12. says — "For the study of Latin one should have 'a right judgment and modest disposition." Saint Mechtilde and Saint Gertrude were well versed in Latin. Louis de Blois says of the latter, *"Brevi tempore multum promovit in cognitione linguae Latinae."* — *Conclav. anim.*, Append. 3, 4.

their falling into vice, by boring them, is perhaps not inconsiderable. Thus, while I seem to be giving you only some advice on literature, I am thinking of, and seeking to attain, another end, and in reality I am giving religious counsels.

Study possesses another great advantage for a woman; it disgusts her with what is useless and frivolous, and with those considerations which sin against almost every Christian virtue; it attaches her to her own home, and preserves her from innumerable dangers. How pleasant it is to sit by the fireside, and read a book which treats of God, of the soul, and of life's duties! Mankind is readily forgotten; intercourse with men is so difficult, often so painful! Whenever the living weary me, says Cardinal de Cheverus, I turn to converse with the dead. Happy dead! whose spirit still breathes in your books; I hold you often far above all living instructors. You have lost your sharp points and angles, if you ever had any; and you only retain your charming wit, so graciously tempered with gentle gravity. You resemble the liqueur of our vicinity which, after detaching all that is hard, thick, and gross from the residue of the vine, takes a form which is spirit almost devoid of matter. How I love to converse with you! And you have another precious quality too, you are not susceptible; when unjustly abandoned through caprice or frivolity, you are not offended, and when again sought, you are as gracious as before. Never has that courtesy which quickly forgets and forgives been carried so far.

"I have never conversed with men," says the author of the *Imitation*, "but I returned less a man to my cell." After certain conversations abroad, have you not often returned home less womanly, less sedate, less amiable, less attentive to your duties? Were you not more frivolous, more dissipated in mind, more attracted by everything dazzling and superficial, more full of vanity and the excessive wish to please? If in place of those useless and often dangerous conversations, you had contrived a quarter or half hour's reading and reflection, you would have felt enkindled in you the spirit of the noble, delicately-minded, exquisitely feeling woman, whose words breathe the perfume of virtue — the spirit of the valiant woman, of the Christian woman. A pagan author advises that women should read the writings of philosophers and the treatises of science. Then, he says, they will no longer be taken up with dances and other frivolities, for their minds will be absorbed in the grand ideas contained in the works of our celebrated writers, and they will be under the influence of a spiritual charm.[1]

In recommending to you the cultivation of literature, I do not advise you to study in the same manner as men. Your mind, like your body, has more suppleness, more flexibility; its mold is more graceful, and there is something about it finer and more exquisite than a man possesses; I speak generally, of course, for we must always count on exceptions. One might say your intellect is more delicate in its perceptions, and sees more easily through the subtle meshes woven around things; if it has less depth, it has usually more quickness; it discerns at a glance, and by a sort of intuition; where man reasons, woman foresees, which caused the Germans to say that you possess somewhat of the spirit of prophecy.[2] Another quality (but with how many defects beside it!) is, that when not on your guard, your head is always led away by your heart. If you love anyone, everything in him must necessarily and at first sight be found perfect, and those who would dare to contradict you on this point are held to be wanting in common sense; if you have taken up some idea, a project, or resolution, and more especially if some predilection of the heart be concerned in them, this idea, this project, this resolution must be, without need of examination, all that is most perfect and desirable, and woe to those who venture to object to it! There, my children, is a point you must carefully watch over, that you may guide yourselves aright. Truth must go before every other consideration, and be the basis of your judgments. Truth before self-love, before our exclusive preferences, before the

[1] Plutarch, *Conjug. præcept.* 48. p. 172, edit. Didot.
[2] Tacitus, *De moribus Germanorum.*

thousand and one passions which agitate the soul like powerful winds. It is the more necessary to guard against this defect, because it is probably one of the principal causes of that versatility which is by no means foreign to woman's nature. Truth is the only solid foundation of convictions and opinions; where it is absent, the fictitious bases we substitute for it soon crumble away. Besides, who can guarantee the impulses of the heart, and hinder its irregular movements, if it be not controlled by principles of truth and by realities? Of itself even, the heart will return at times to truth, to the discomfiture of its passions.

In pointing out the qualities and defects which appertain to the peculiar nature of your minds, I am giving you the rules which should guide you in the choice and method of your studies. Each flower in the same garden opens in a different manner; so should you too develop yourselves in this vast garden of science and literature according to the nature of your minds, and the kind of fruit you are meant to bear. If God has created you a lowly violet, do not seek to imitate a lofty shrub; if you are the lily in all its dazzling whiteness, do not aspire to the gigantic girth of the stately oak; that is to say, let your studies be proportioned to your capacity, to the nature of your calling, and to the character of your minds, and do not try to be learned after the fashion of men. Every being in creation preserves its own tints while reflecting the rays of the sun. Thus, you will cull the roses of knowledge without having to endure the thorns, particularly those poisoned ones which infuse into the mind a pestilential venom, from the effects of which it is difficult to free one's self entirely.

Saint Clement of Alexandria enumerates in one of his works the Grecian ladies who had occupied themselves with the study of literature, science, and philosophy. The beginning of the chapter has a special application to the subject of which we treat. This father wishes to prove that women as well as men are capable of attaining perfection, and he seems to desire that they should devote themselves to study, in order to fill up this sketch of a perfect life. "The daughters of Didorus," he says, "excelled in logic; . . . many women followed the courses given by Plato; Aspasia's lectures were not useless to Socrates; and I do not count the women who have excelled in poetry and painting."[1] In another place he draws the following conclusion —"The study of philosophy is therefore a duty for women as well as for men, although the latter, by their superiority, occupy the foremost rank;"[2] and we know that the ancients, and Saint Clement of Alexandria in particular, understood by philosophy, the study of every science as well as the presence of every virtue. In the *Acts of Saint Catherine* we read that she was acquainted with sacred and profane literature; she herself testified to it before her judges — "I have applied myself," she tells them, "to every branch of rhetoric, philosophy, geometry, and other sciences."[3]

Saint Monica is another admirable model for you in this respect. She loved to discuss the highest problems of philosophy with Saint Augustine and his companions; and she did so with a breadth of view and elevation of thought which astonished her hearers. Having entered her son's apartment one day while some very deep questions were being argued, she asked the subject of the conversation. Saint Augustine bade his secretary relate it. "Oh!" exclaimed Saint Monica, "you have never seen women take a part in this sort of discussion." "I pay no heed to the opinions of fools and arrogant men," replied Saint Augustine. "Rest satisfied, mother, that many people will rejoice to hear that you share in my philosophic studies; they will be more pleased at that than if we applied ourselves to any other grave or recreative pursuit, for among the ancients many

---

[1] *Stromat.* 1. 4. cap. 19.
[2] *Stromat.* cap. 8. pp. 1331-1334, 1275, edit. Migné.
[3] *Omnem externam et nostram scripturam perlegerat.* . . . *Sum exercitata in omni disciplinâ rhetoricæ, et philosophiæ, geometricæ, et aliarum scientiarum* — "She had read all sacred and profane literature." . . . "I have applied myself to every branch of rhetoric, philosophy, geometry, and the other sciences." — See Surius, November 25.

Third Discourse

women studied philosophy, and your ideas always particularly delight me." Saint Augustine goes on to point out to his mother all that was powerful, noble, and philosophical in her character. Saint Monica tries to stop him by declaring that he has never before said so much that was false, or with so amiable a motive. On another similar occasion Saint Monica spoke with so much admiration and earnestness, and her words created so deep an impression, that we forgot, says Saint Augustine, it was a woman who spoke, and thought we were listening to some illustrious philosopher.[1]

But nothing can be more sublime or beautiful than the colloquy of Saint Augustine and Saint Monica by the sea-shore at Ostia. A few days later and Saint Augustine was to lose her whom he so tenderly loved; therefore it was in reality, though unsuspected by them, the dying song of the swan. They were alone, leaning against a window, contemplating the boundless. "Our conversation," says Saint Augustine, "was full of ineffable sweetness, for forgetting the past, and ardently looking forward to the future, we spoke of the magnificent destiny awaiting us. . . . Carried aloft by a sudden transport of love towards the Infinite Being, our hearts soared beyond space, beyond the firmament above our heads, and sought the Incarnate Wisdom. We were conversing thus, when in a moment, inflamed by love, we felt as though, in one bound of exultant rapture, we had actually attained the Eternal Wisdom, the object of all our desires; at His feet we laid the first fruits of our souls, and then descended again to earth, where the sound of our human voices was being heard. But how poor are the words of men! What resemblance can they have, O my God, to Thy Supreme Word?"[2]

This magnificent dialogue between Saint Augustine and his mother is accompanied by the most sublime reflections on time and eternity, on the creation and its connection with an omnipotent God. It is one of the best proofs that women are

---

[1] *De Beatâ Vitâ*, t. 1. cap. 10. p. 504, edit. Gaume.
[2] *Confessions*, 1. 9. cap. 10.

fully able to take their part in the school of a vast and grand philosophy, and even that the ecstasies of that philosophy may be enjoyed by them: by ecstasy I mean that hour of calm and intense rapture when the soul, detached from itself, seems to see the "face to face" of which Saint Paul speaks.

Perhaps I ought, before concluding, to have spoken a word to you on reading; but I should not now have time to treat the subject suitably; and probably at a future day, in the course of these our monthly meetings, I shall find an occasion to revert to it. I trust that today I have succeeded in steering safely through the Straits of Messina, keeping mid-channel, and not inclining too much to either side. I do not wish to make you learned women in the sense which excites derision, but I do desire that nothing which elevates the mind and ennobles the heart should be unknown to you. A woman's soul has the same origin as a man's, and needs light no less than his. This divine plant should not remain uncultivated, but should be made to bring forth fruits, which, though differing in kind from those plucked in the garden of man, are not less excellent if they are properly matured. A prudent infusion of knowledge into a woman's mind can never be injurious to her, for it brings her ideas into right order, and is often the only thing wanting to some people; it rectifies the judgment, strengthens the will, promotes a more dignified and assured line of conduct. May you then, my children, having rendered your fingers deft with the spinning-wheel and the needle, make your minds equally competent to sustain a serious conversation on grave subjects, and to comprehend those books which treat of great and noble ideas. Join to this what Fénelon so aptly styles the modesty of science in women, and you will deserve to have applied to you, also, the words of Holy Writ which formed my text of today—"Such is a wise and silent woman, and there is nothing so much worth as a well instructed soul."

Fourth Discourse
The Valiant Woman pilots her vessel with grace and fortitude through stormy seas.

She is like the merchant's ship: she bringeth her bread from afar.
(Prov. 31, 14)

MY CHILDREN,

A woman should attend diligently to her household affairs; it is one of her principal duties. She will never degrade herself by condescending to the smallest details, for there is a manner of doing so which compromises neither her dignity, authority, nor character. We daily see the sun, without losing aught of its brilliancy or splendid majesty, penetrating everywhere, and illuminating even the meanest and poorest spots. Manual labor, of whatever nature — whether the spinning of wool or flax, handling the distaff or the needle, superintending the making of dishes or of garments — manual labor, I repeat, is always one of the best and most useful resources in a woman's life; and one of the plague-spots of our present epoch is its being utterly laid aside, or at least, rarely practiced. Does this mean that intellectual labors should be abandoned, and a woman's part limited to superintending cookery and knitting stockings? I think we fully established the contrary by pointing out the medium to be observed between these extremes. Without wishing to transform you into blue-stockings, which is but a ridiculous character and injurious in many points of view; without wishing to oblige all women to study, which to many would be an impossibility, I still maintain that study, in a suitable degree, is most desirable for the greater number of women, and it is easy to corroborate this maxim by the opinions of grave authorities, and in particular by the example of the mother of Saint Augustine.

We will now proceed with the explanation of the book of *Proverbs*, always taking the verses in order of succession.

"She is like the merchant's ship, she bringeth her bread from afar."

Woman is like unto a ship! This idea of Holy Writ appears to me so beautiful and so rich in suggestions of grace and truth, that I shall ask your permission to pause here awhile, and even to devote the entire of this discourse to it. I shall also venture to call this exhortation exclusively "Rochelais," for it has been composed by the aid of recollections of my sea-side walks.

Behold yonder vessel so skillfully built; it possesses beauty and strength alike, and as it speeds forth over the waters with its flowing sails and graceful form, it is one of the chief ornaments of the sea. Seen from afar, you might take it for some gigantic bird with extended wings, floating over the surface of the liquid plain. But it is not sufficient for the vessel to be graceful, it must also be solidly built, or it will soon become the prey of the waves; the smallest billows will shatter it, the first gales sink it. Therefore, the timber has been selected and wrought with the utmost care, each part joined together by a combination of accomplished skill; and if the ship be intended for service in the far-off seas, it is often covered with galvanized iron, that it may be able to withstand every shock, and be preserved from the rust and decay induced by the contact of the water. Marvellous portrait of the valiant woman! She too is graceful like a well-built ship; her speech, her motions, her gait, everything about her, partakes of the majestic port and softly-gliding motions of a ship. She is an ornament to her family and to society, and in worldly assemblies presents an

Fourth Discourse

image of those graceful yawls, so much admired in our port, and whose history and origin we are now seeking to know. She is the living exemplification of the text — "A gracious woman shall find glory."[1] But beauty by itself is useless, may even become dangerous; therefore the valiant woman, like the ship, possesses strength; of a vigorous Christian temperament, she can resist the utmost fury of the sea, brave the tempestuous waves, and hold her course amidst the stormy billows; she, too, is fortified with galvanized metal, that is to say, with those solid virtues which can withstand the assaults of the passions. Though she may have to abide in troubled waters, exposed to all the dangers of life, she still rests intact, and ever proudly maintains the honor of her name and house.

A ship has many sails, of different size and shape, and placed in different positions; it has some for every point of the wind, and these are employed according to circumstances, with ingenious skill. Sometimes they are all extended in billowy folds, presenting an exquisitely beautiful object to the spectator's eye; while at others, they seem to be carefully husbanded, and only brought forth at particular times. Should the winds prove contrary, the ship profits by that very opposition to attain her ends; she maneuvers adroitly, seems to turn aside from her path, then tacks, and so forces the astonished wind to favor her cause. Should no breath of air be stirring, and the calm sea present only a motionless surface, the ship makes use of a power which science has placed at her disposal; she gets up steam, a strange motion thrills through the vessel, and the amazed sea is compelled to open a broad, deep furrow for her passage. The valiant woman has likewise her sails of mind and heart; she possesses a number of resources which, combined in all honor, uprightness, and probity, serve to guide her course through the ever difficult navigation of the affairs of this world. When the wind is favorable, she moves forward with all sails set, letting the breeze of prosperity conduct her to the desired end; but, like a prudent pilot, she still keeps her eye on the

[1] *Prov.* 11:16.

wind, and confides as little in the stability of the things of this world, as the sailor does in the constancy of the waves. As soon as she perceives a modification in men or things, she shapes her course accordingly, but always preserving the integrity of an upright mind; she varies her combinations, and furls the sails which have become useless, or even dangerous. Should the wind turn altogether contrary, the valiant woman alters her mode of steering, and gets her ship into a different position; although she has confidence in the strength of the vessel, and in the stout texture of her sails, yet she does not rashly fight against the full power of the storm; she takes up her position midway, where she can tack and compel the wind to blow obliquely on her sails with abated violence, with a force too feeble to overwhelm the ship, yet powerful enough to impel her precisely in the opposite direction. And again, should the wind fall suddenly, and the vessel's progress be checked by another mischance, that of a dead calm, the valiant woman has recourse to steam, that is, to her own energetic mind and the vigor of a well-balanced character. What I wish to infer is, that woman, with all her delicacy of mind, docility of character, flexibility of nature, quickness of apprehension, and prophetic intuition of heart, can, if she will, put all these resources at the call of virtue and good sense, extricate herself from all perplexities and false positions, and, by degrees, compel the contrary winds to do her justice and second her efforts.

But in order to accomplish this, my children, you must belong to the order of valiant women; you must know how to possess yourselves in the assured strength of moral courage; you must have something almost manlike in your characters. Woman too often loses her head in the midst of a tempest; she falls into a swoon, or she rages and storms as loudly as the waves themselves, and during these faintings or these outbursts, the vessel founders.

Let us not yet grow weary of contemplating our graceful ship. It has a rare and very precious quality, that of balancing itself upon the waters; it possesses a power of elasticity which enables it to follow the waves, to rise and fall with them, yet always continuing its own course. It takes this way rather than that of fighting directly against the force of the sea; it prefers these yielding movements to the violence which would precipitate it against the waves, rudely seeking to carve for itself a passage through them. I recommend to your consideration, my children, this power of balancing yourselves upon the waves; it is the best of all tactics in many circumstances. Yes, very often the best and surest and most perfect way is to let the billows of trials and difficulties come and go, and toss about the vessel of our life at their will, while we tranquilly exclaim with the Wise Man — "But Thy providence, O Father, governeth it: for Thou hast made a way even in the sea, and a most sure path among the waves. Showing that Thou art able to save out of all things, yea, though a man went to sea without art."[1] Having recited this prayer of the mariner, it is often best to do nothing one's self, but wait and follow the motion of the waves, not even seeking to divert them from their course. Only we must always carefully preserve that suppleness and buoyancy which have hitherto kept us afloat on the waters; we must give up none of our real convictions or good habits, but leave ourselves to drift at the will of God, while waiting for better days. Nothing disconcerts human waves so much as this attitude: they comprehend in the end that there is nothing to be gained by attacking certain vessels, and, resigning themselves to the rate of being unheeded, are more quickly calmed. True piety, deeply rooted in the heart, can alone give you this combined buoyancy and energy which holds its ground all the better for appearing to yield. But what seems so simple, natural, and necessary to be done in this respect, is extremely difficult in practice. It costs self-love a great price to reach this point; at each moment sacrifices are demanded — sacrifices of our thoughts and affections, perpetual immolations of our own wishes; vanity is wounded, feelings hurt, and every susceptibility aroused. No; nature left to herself could never produce these effects, so

[1] Wis. 14:3, 4.

simple, so easy of acquirement, so necessary to happiness; at the utmost, she can only sometimes appreciate their ideal beauty; but self-love will have its revolts, and becomes the worst of counselors; it refuses to yield, it chooses rather to resist openly, and bear the deplorable consequences of its obstinacy. True piety, detaching us from the things of this world, raising us above the earth, and elevating our whole character, naturally predisposes us to that firm, vigorous, well-balanced state of mind in which prudence is taken as ballast, and the impetuous movements of self-love are restrained by a superior wisdom.

Our ship has yet another resource: when the weather becomes too bad, it casts anchor. The anchor is a weighty piece of iron, bent back at both ends, and suspended from the side of the vessel; this, in stormy seas, when there might be danger in continuing the course, is let go. The ponderous mass falls into the deep, fastens down the ship by its weight, and becomes a kind of solid foundation for it in the depths of the sea. Our soul should also be provided with its anchor — nay, with many anchors suspended from the bulwarks; and when the storm comes, she should drop them into the depths of God's providence, and rest unmoved, awaiting the end of the tempest. The anchors of the soul are many and various, for under that name I would place everything tending to support and consolidate it; such as good and well-established principles, great firmness of character, safe and pious friendships, and, above all, unshaken confidence in God, and energetic faith, capable of moving mountains. These are the real anchors of the soul, and when the chain which holds them has been forged in heaven, it cannot break. Ladies, amid the numerous difficulties of family life, amid those heavy ground-swells which arise so unexpectedly, tossing about in all directions the vessel of the soul, follow this counsel: cast anchor and remain quiet. And after that, you ask. Nothing more, only keep your anchor firm, and pray. Is this not what the pilot does at sea?

Fourth Discourse

A ship always carries a mariner's compass, and by the aid of this little instrument it can tell where it is, and whither its course is tending, for the magnetic needle points out the position and direction of the vessel. In many circumstances the stars might serve the same purpose, and the polar star is our surest indication of the north; but sometimes clouds cover the sky and the stars are hidden; the compass then becomes indispensable, and replaces for our guidance the light of the heavens.

It is still more necessary that we should possess a compass in life, a celestial guide to keep us from losing our way. The gravest misfortune to many women has been their want of a compass in certain events of their lives, and especially in youth. The storm came, darkness thickened round them, and ignorant of where their path was leading them, they were shipwrecked on the rocks. A steady, mild, enlightened piety will always prove a woman's best compass; the light of faith should direct her way, and in her inmost soul she should have a far-seeing prudence, a heavenly instinct, an upright conscience, which may serve to guide her aright through the gloom, and point out the true bearings of surrounding objects. With these precautions, my children, you will not veer about at the mercy of every wind of doctrine, and you will know that there are paths no Christian woman should tread, and rocks which must be shunned if shipwreck would be avoided. The mariner's compass may be also taken in another sense. There are minds who either have no compass, or have put it out of order, and with them the north is to be found in the south, the east in the west, and very often they see everything upside down. To use a sailor's expression, they are always losing the north; nothing with them is fixed, nothing steady; perpetual instability, repeated tackings, as frequent as they are inopportune, so that one may say of them, that they are constant to nothing but inconstancy. What advice can we give them? For religion must have counsel for every situation of life, and every diversity of character. The practice of humility would be of a special utility to them; a profound diffidence of themselves and their own opinions, a prudent deliberation in their resolutions and acts, would preserve them from many dangers, and prevent many false steps. I would also advise such to have themselves taken in tow by some other vessel duly fitted with a compass and steered by a skilful pilot — that is, to let themselves be guided and directed by sensible, attached friends, and to do nothing without their advice. Thus will their natural incapacity be supplemented as much as is possible; and without this indispensable precaution, the number of their shipwrecks will be incalculable.

Let us proceed with the inspection of our ship. What are those great, bare trees called, which seem to start up in the middle? I can count one, two, three, principal ones. They are the props which sustain the ropes, the sails, and all the rigging of the vessel. If the ship's masts give way, her strength is gone, she struggles but feebly against the force of the waves, and is often on the verge of foundering. In like manner, it is necessary that our minds should be furnished with those vigorous thoughts, those fixed principles, which may be termed the scaffolding of moral life; and I do not mean this counsel to apply to religious matters only, but to all things connected with man's life, to temporal affairs, and to the rules which should guide our conduct in our dealings with men and things. Principles are needed everywhere; I do not say systematic rules, for a system is always dangerous, and often a cause of imprudent acts, and more or less grave faults; but those principles, which, without ever once straying from the line of truth, yet possess sufficient elasticity to adapt themselves to all the requirements of prudence and charity. They are the props of life, the masts of the human vessel; around them are grouped and twined the thoughts, the projects, the resolutions of the soul — all the various threads which weave the net-work of life. Woe to the soul devoid of masts! Without power of resistance, she can never win her way through the heavy sea of contradictions and opposing currents; her progress will be irregular and wavering, like a ship beaten about by contrary winds.

Neither are masts all-sufficient; a helm is also needed. This is a small piece of wood half-hidden in the water. The pilot, almost imperceptibly, communicates to it a perpetually changing motion when in dangerous places, and this movement of the helm is the true guiding power of the ship, giving it an impulse which can, at any moment, vary and incline its course in an opposite direction. Thus impelled by a prudent, intelligent hand, the ship sails safely on in the midst of perils.

The soul needs her helm also — I mean that spirit of large-minded, enlightened prudence, which, with a glance, embraces the horizon, discerns the difficulties of the way, and takes that direct line onwards which, without ever deviating from the paths of truth and uprightness, can yet shape itself according to circumstances, inclining now to the right, now to the left, and making life a succession of broken lines, yet still maintaining a direct course.

Is this enough for the safety of the vessel? No; the ship of the stoutest build, well manned, with strong masts, good sails, and helm ably handled, may yet founder after a few days' or hours' sailing; for it is also necessary that the pilot should be perfectly conversant with the sea and its shores, the depth of the soundings, the position of rocks and sand-banks, the power of the winds, and the direction of the currents; in a word, that he should be thoroughly acquainted with what is termed nautical science. For that purpose, he is provided with a chart where everything is marked. He knows that at such a point he has to encounter a difficulty, perhaps a headland, against which the sea breaks furiously; or a sunken rock, where the vessel may go to pieces; or a sand-bank, where she may be engulfed; or an under-current to suck her down. You too, my children, should have a chart of the most dangerous and stormy of all seas, the sea of life. I will explain my meaning. Learn, as far as is possible, the strong and the weak points of your surroundings; do not hug certain coasts, or you will be bruised and buffeted by

The Valiant Woman

the rocks; beware of certain straits between men or things which you are required to pass. There are treacherous currents in such a place, the more dangerous that nothing announces their presence. Further on is a sand-bank. What means that, you ask. It is beside you: it is that man, or that woman, in whom perhaps you most confide. Trust them not, I beg of you; they are but a sand-bank, not firm land; your bark will sink therein, and once sunk, it may not be easy to raise it again. There are some persons whom we cannot shake off when we wish, if once we have ventured among their treacherous shoals; they are not unlike the Firth of Maumusson,[1] where, if ships once touch the bottom, they are drawn down by a relentless force which loses none of its power by its slow operation. You are coasting a certain shore, you are frequenting certain company, you say the wind is entirely favorable. It is just possible you are deceived. The wind, it is true, blows in your favor when you are present; but only turn your back, and then ask some honest sailor who has stayed on shore, and he will tell you that your words, your actions, your very remembrance has been assailed by a cold and biting north-easter. What still remains to be told? In the sea are fish with formidable rows of teeth who snap up the unfortunate swimmer at the moment he least expects, because these fierce creatures always keep between two currents. There are also characters who keep themselves concealed beneath water; to use an expression of Saint Gregory Nazianzen, "The Armenians," he says, "are neither candid nor simple, they are wholly crafty, and resemble sunken rocks."[2] Probably you have never known of the existence of these men-fishes; you will only begin to suspect it when they have reached you with their cruel fangs, the more dangerous, because unseen; for they are hidden under water if in the sea, or beneath velvet if on land — for these creatures are amphibious, and we meet them by land and sea.

But I must return to our ship. Will you descend with me into her interior? How admirably everything is disposed!

[1] A Strait between the Isle of Oleron and the coast of Marennes.
[2] *Orat. 43*. n. 17, t. 2. p. 518, edit. Migné.

Fourth Discourse

What prudent arrangements! What cleanliness! What good order in saloons, decks, and cabins! The captain attends himself to everything, and perfect order reigns throughout. No encumbering heaps of merchandise, no disturbance among passengers, and the crew, though many, obey like one man. So is the mind of the valiant woman; inspect its numerous compartments with me. Wisdom is captain of the vessel, and all is in good order: thoughts, desires, projects, and resolutions. All the internal machinery performs its work with marvellous simplicity; the steam of the imagination is safely regulated, everything is in its place, and we may truly say that the chief beauty of this soul is in the interior. Compare her soul with that of others, and see the difference! If one could visit their interiors, torch in hand, what gloomy spots we should discover, what disorder throughout! The most dissimilar objects are heaped together, the strangest ideas intermingled, the most whimsical wishes sought to be combined; in one word, it is a picture of supreme disorder and entire absence of all regularity; and we might say that such minds lived in the constant bustle of a removal.

I have not finished the explanation of my text — "The valiant woman is like the merchant's ship, she bringeth her bread from afar." It is not enough that the ship should be well equipped, fitted with masts, sails, and steam, and having on board an experienced pilot, thoroughly acquainted with the sea and its dangers: she must also obtain a cargo. Accordingly, she starts; she sails for India or America, and returns laden with merchandise. So ought the valiant woman to enrich her family by her cares, her attention, her economy, her constant vigilance; these constitute her commerce, her voyages, her legitimate trade. We see merchants amass considerable fortunes from small profits; for little by little the grains of sand increase, each wave brings some with it, and at length the shore is covered; each drop of water falls without evaporation into the cistern, and the quantity soon grows considerable. A woman may also arrive at astonishing results by care, watchfulness, and strict, though not penurious, economy; at the end of each month, even of each week, she may enter the harbor of her family with an unexpected prize.

But, my children, there is something besides money in life. What moral and intellectual wealth may not the valiant woman glean in her daily intercourse with other minds, especially with grave, Christian souls? She skims off the cream of conversations, lectures, and reading; she carries on a rich piracy in intellectual seas, for that is a noble and perfectly honorable trade. And when she returns to her family, she dispenses to them her plunder; she opens the hold of her vessel, and her children hasten to share in the booty, like the merchant's family who are awaiting a rich cargo which America has dispatched to them; or still more, like those cabin-boys we see watching for the arrival of home-bound ships, and seizing on them as a prey to which they have some right. Thus from all points of view, both of material and intellectual riches, the valiant woman does indeed resemble the merchant's ship, who bringeth her treasures from afar.

One of the prettiest sights I have seen at Rochelle has been, during my early morning walks, when I sometimes beheld a fleet of tiny boats leaving the harbor and spreading over the sea; one might imagine they were ranging themselves in line of battle against some unknown enemy, whose approach had just been signalled to them; happily the flotilla is only directed against small fish. The effect is exquisite; the little streamers, the varied colors, the flowing sails, the buoyant motion of these tiny barks — everything, in a word, contributes to charm the eye. These miniature fleets sail away, and return laden with spoils.

Let these be an image of you, ladies; graceful barks, sail away in battle order; go fish for souls; let material help be the bait used by your hearts, and the souls of your brethren the fruit of your fishing. It will be always sweet and consoling to me to see you thus set forth, and await your return on the shore, praising God for the good you will have done to our much-loved poor, and beseeching Him to return it to you a hundred-fold.

Fifth Discourse
Sleep and counsels of the night...

She hath risen in the night. (Prov. 31:15)

MY CHILDREN,

The valiant woman resembles a ship in its beauty, grace, and strength. Like her, too, she has numerous sails, which she varies according to time and circumstance; and in her are also to be found all the resources of an alert, intelligent mind, which she knows how to combine in a thousand different ways, and in such a manner as never to run counter to the wind; but by tacking prudently to compel it to oppose no longer the course of her vessel, and even to accelerate her progress. She does not seek to force her way violently through the billows, but prefers to follow their movement, rising and falling with them, and balancing herself on the waters, oscillating more or less rapidly, it is true, but still always with a gentler motion than would be the shock of rough, precipitate rushing onwards in a direct line. Should storms rage furiously, her anchors are let drop into the sea, and become her safeguards against the fury of the waves. These anchors are confidence in God, fixed principles deeply imbued with a Christian spirit, and great firmness of character.

Our beauteous bark is also provided with a mariner's compass, to direct her course amid the obscurity of the night, to point out the surest path through dangers, and to correct the wanderings of a disordered imagination. She is also fitted with stout, strong masts, to bear up and sustain all the ropes and sails which ordinarily compose the fittings of a vessel.

Let this ship be launched with a careful steersman and an able captain, and furnished with a correct and minute chart of the seas they sail in; let her internal accommodations be well appointed, without luxury, but with comfort tempered by simplicity, and she will pass safely through the dangers of the ocean, and return home laden with rich merchandise.

This, then, my children, is a true symbol of woman's life, as appropriate as it is beautiful; and we studied it closely at our last meeting. Our task in the two following instructions will not be such an easy one; nevertheless, we will undertake it, even at the risk of stranding our bark. Its matter is naturally suggested by the words of the text — "*She hath risen in the night.*" Let us, then, consider sleep and the questions pertaining to it. We shall commence the subject in today's, and conclude it in next month's lecture.

The life of man is a constant warfare, an arduous trial, and a long struggle, in which his strength becomes exhausted. How often at the end of the day are we tempted to cry out with the Prophet — "Why is light given to him that is in misery, and life to them that are in bitterness of soul?"[1] An ever-fatherly providence foresaw this daily weariness and fatigue, and provided for us a renovating bath each night, from which we seem to derive new life. After a profound, sweet sleep, man rises again, imbued with the strength and vigor of youth. His body is full of life, his heart is refreshed, the air seems lighter, and his chest more dilated to inhale it. Sleep, says the great English poet —

> . . . Knits up the ravell'd sleeve of care:
> The death of each day's life, sore labor's bath,
> Balm of hurt minds, great Nature's second course,
> Chief nourisher in life's feast.[2]

---

[1] Job 3: 20.
[2] *Macbeth*, act ii. scene 2.

Fifth Discourse

An ancient philosopher said that sleep assured the success of medicine; that it was the deliverer of captives, the desire of the sick, the comfort of the afflicted, repose to the mind, the universal habit of rich and poor, and the longing of each returning night.[1] Thence this exclamation of the ancient choruses —" O Sleep, thou who ignorest pain and care, come to us with all thy charms; thou king of calm and happiness, thou healer of men!"[2]

Nothing is truer than this description of the salutary influence and beneficent action of sleep. Without it the prescriptions of physicians would be of no avail, and the worn-out body be impervious to all the power of their art. A good night will often effect more than all the visits of the most skilful doctors; but this truth, drawn from experience, does not take from the practical utility of medical science. Sleep brings temporary freedom, at least, to the captive. It releases him from the exigences of his organs, from the prison of his body; he hears no more the cries and continual demands of those jailers we call the senses; he lives in another world. It is true that in the morning he must return to his chain, but after a good sleep, even that seems lighter, and the prisoner himself feels stronger to bear it. Are you ill? Ill rather in mind than in body? Call sleep to your aid. It will drown your cares in its peaceful depths; and even though you should encounter them again, rising above the waters, at least there will have been a wholesome interruption of them, by which suffering is deprived of its most painful attribute — continuity. Sleep is the wealth of the poor, as it is of the rich man: indeed, I would even call it the special inheritance of the poor. He sleeps better because he has worked harder, and nature, always just, repays him more abundantly. He sleeps better because he lives more temperately, and his stomach is therefore less charged with those fumes which mount to the brain, agitate the nerves and the blood, and turn into an oven the refreshing bath which Providence

[1] *Fragment. Phil. Græc.* p. 514, edit. Didot.
[2] Sophocles, *Philoctetes*, v. 827.

has prepared for us.[1] Sleep is a gift which seems ever new and never produces satiety, if used in moderation. We weary of everything, even of what is best. We quickly tire of dinner-parties, balls, amusement, conversation; but each recurring evening the thought of our bed is an ever-smiling apparition, and no vision of cooling bath amid the fiery heats of summer can give more pleasure. Saint Chrysostom has left us a reflection on sleep, which is replete with charm and love and Christian poetry — "When mothers wish to put their little ones to sleep, they take and rock them gently in their arms, then hide them away under curtains, and leave them quiet. So does Providence spread darkness as an immense veil over the world, and invite men to rest from their labors."[2]

The Grecian philosopher also says that night brings wisdom to the wakeful, and that sleep is the image of death. Have you ever sleepless nights? Do not fear them over much, for perhaps that is the hour when God will speak to you. During the day, the soul is drawn away by exterior objects. She sees and hears nothing; her ears are spell-bound by the sirens who surround her. How can she distinguish the words of true wisdom? The voice of God, says the prophet, is heard when the night is in the middle of her course.[3] The clouds break, the serene light of truth appears to us: we behold it, and its beams are so bright and searching that we can no longer doubt. We have not always the strength to follow this divine light, but it is still something to have seen it. The vision of it is a seed deposited in the soul, which may become developed in some unexpected circumstance. Night brings counsel, says the proverb. It brings counsel, because it calms down many things, and then the soul, in the stillness and quiet of nocturnal reflection, can form wiser resolutions. Night will bring all the more counsel if you charm the hours of sleeplessness by

[1] A witness above suspicion has said, — "The poor sleep more soundly on their straw, than the rich on their magnificent couches." — M. de Maintenon, *Lettres sur l'Education*, p. 5, edit. Lavallée.
[2] *De Compunct.* 1. ii. n. 5, t. i. p. 182.
[3] Wis. 18:14.

Fifth Discourse

the thought of God. Prayer is the night-lamp which should be ever beside us, that when we wake, it may speak to us of heaven. I know not what mysterious harmony exists between night and prayer, but the saints have ever held it to be the best time for prayer. One would say that the dew of heaven chose the same hours to fall on souls in which the terrestrial dew gathers to refresh plants. At night all is silent; the noises of earth have ceased; peace reigns around, and then the soul discerns her God more clearly, and can converse with Him in those mysterious and familiar colloquies which recall the loving intercourse of two friends who have met, apart from the crowd, in order to converse more freely together. Wonderful intercourse of the soul with her God! It is part of the life of the saints. All the tenderest and deepest emotions of the heart love the shroud of mystery! And thus, when all creation is covered by the veil of night, and the soul alone is waking in the divine light, what ineffable happiness, what exquisite pleasure to converse with God, to lay before Him all the secrets of our hearts, to receive His holy inspirations, "to speak to Him face to face, as a friend is wont to speak to his friend."[1]

Try to partake sometimes, my children, of this divine ambrosia of night; it is the most delicious banquet for the heart, the brightest light of the soul. "Night," says Saint Clement of Alexandria, "is styled by the Greeks the good counsellor, because then the soul, disengaged from the empire of the senses, retires within herself, to listen attentively to the inspirations of wisdom."[2] May providence ever grant you the blessing of good nights! If, however, sickness or grief should ever come to destroy your rest, then do I wish you, in all fatherly affection, a result similar to that which is so well described by a celebrated woman. "He (God) was the chief object of my thoughts by night as well as by day, because for a long time past my infirmities have rarely permitted me to sleep more than an hour and a half together, and have often

---
[1] Ex. 33:11
[2] *Strom.* 1. iv. cap. xxii. t. i. p. 1351.

forced me to leave my bed fifteen or twenty times in the night, and to walk about my room the greater part of the time. The benedictions which God showered on those bad nights, as the world calls them, are indescribable."[1] It is of such delicious moments that Saint Ambrose says, "These are the excellent nights, the luminous nights full of stars."[2] Happy the souls who rise to contemplate them!

Sleep is an image of death. Nothing is truer, sweeter, or sadder than this thought. Look at that sleeping man; he is far away for many long hours; his soul seems to have gone on a journey; it has gone as the dead go; the time of its return is the only difference. The body itself is lying as it will lie some day in the tomb. The eyes are closed, the features are motionless; and but for that little sound of breathing, which seems the last frail link to the soul, the illusion would be complete: for have you ever contemplated the just man on his bed of death? He, too, seems to sleep; the calm of the features, the serenity of the face, the sweet expression of the countenance; in a word, all the beauty of a living being is there — breath alone is wanting. Therefore did the ancients call sleep and death by the same name; they called it a withdrawal of the soul — a withdrawal which in sleep is temporary, in death, eternal. "The man who is dead," says Heraclitus, "borders on sleep because he is deprived of light; and the living man who sleeps touches

---

[1] Madame Swetchine, *Lettres à la Princesse Galitzin*, t. i. p. 460.

"I think of the Trappists who are rising at night to pray, of the sick who are counting every hour in pain, of the afflicted who are weeping, of the dead who are sleeping, cold and stiff, on their couches. Oh! what serious thoughts night brings with it! I cannot believe that the wicked man, the scoffer, the infidel, can feel as obstinate by night as by day." — *Journal de Mademoiselle Eugénie de Guérin*.

Madame Swetchine says elsewhere: "In the long nights of the Polar regions, a light sometimes appears, resembling the dawn, which dissipates the darkness in an instant; so in our advanced years, instinctive illuminations, which seem to belong to a new day, strike on our vision. Those wakeful hours of night have done me much good, for it was seldom indeed that these valued friends did not bring me the benefit of some heavenly thought or feeling." — Œuvres, t. ii. p. 216.

[2] *Epist.* 22. n. 8.

the regions of death; even the blind man bears some relation to him who slumbers."[1] Thus from blindness to sleep, and from sleep to death, there is a gradual transition, and the world of the living is linked to that of the dead by an uninterrupted chain. As sleep, then, is the image of death — even its twin brother, as old Homer calls it[2] — never lie down on your beds, my children, without making this solemn reflection: "One day, and perhaps a day that is near at hand, I, too, shall be lying in death, and, it may be, on this very bed. My friends and neighbors will be weeping around my lifeless body; they will still call on me, but my soul will have gone on its last great journey — it will be before its judge." Make this reflection when you lie down each evening, make it when you wake in the night, and then will the night truly become a good counsellor unto you; each evening you will listen to an excellent sermon, and the night will often prove the best and most eloquent of preachers.

It was essential, in order to arrive afterwards at my conclusions, to show that I was no enemy to sleep, and I was even bound to give it all the praise it so justly merits. Sleep is a boon granted by Providence to soul and body; it is our best physician, and the restorer of moral and physical strength. Even its very interruptions become a period of refreshment, of peace, and of fruitful calm; but the very best things may be abused, and because sleep is excellent, we must not therefore conclude that we may give ourselves up to it, without further reflection, in all security and confidence. Sleep would then become as treacherous an enemy as wine.

Now we touch on delicate ground, and in an instant I find myself near those Straits of Messina which I mentioned in a former discourse. Obliged to comment on a particular text of Scripture, and to annotate it with reflections founded on faith and reason, I yet run a risk of displeasing a portion of my audience, and perhaps of preaching to the winds. I

---

[1] Quoted by Saint Clement of Alexandria, *Strom. L* iv. cap. xxii., p. 1351.
[2] *Iliad*, xiv. 231.

hope, however, you will bear the difficulties of my position in mind, and that those amongst you who do not relish a practical acceptance of my doctrine will at least allow that its tenets are founded on truth and your own best interests. I do not ask of you to grant me more at present.

Before laying down a series of propositions on sleep, I make every needful exception in favor of the sick, of the suffering, and of persons of weak constitution, always provided that the mantle of night be not too much enlarged to cover all the ingenious excuses of sloth disguised under the form of pretended infirmities. For it might happen that a person will remain in bed eight mornings successively to get rid of the effects of a sick headache, and then, to prevent its recurrence, she will remain in bed eight mornings more. And so if the indisposition return every fortnight, sloth will find its reign firmly established.

Medicine teaches that when we have once passed the age in which our constitution is being formed, six or seven hours' sleep is generally sufficient. Prolonged slumbers have many disadvantages. The blood grows thick, and the whole organization is sluggish. The mind suffers — it becomes indolent and heavy, and incapable of sacrifices; grown weak and enervated, it indulges in effeminate idleness, until its every movement partakes of the inconveniences and slowness of repletion. She is saturated with sleep, to use the expression of one of the ancients, "*Somno saginati.*"[1] When we sleep too much our ideas become torpid as well as our limbs, our activity of soul and body is blunted, and we end by being always in a state of semi-somnolence, even in our waking hours. Therefore, great sleepers can never accomplish much, the larger portion of their existence being given to sleep, and the rest of it passed in habitual drowsiness. Listen to two very different authorities, who, by their very diversity, have considerable weight. "Excessive sleep," says Plato, "is not salutary either for mind or body; it is incompatible with the occupations of life. During sleep we are good for nothing, no more than if we

---

[1] Pliny, *Hist. Nat. 1.* viii. n. 54.

were dead. Whoever wishes for a sound body and clear mind must prolong his waking hours as much as possible, taking only that quantity of sleep which is necessary for health, and very little is enough when we have once formed a good habit."[1] "The young girl," writes Fénelon, "has accustomed herself to sleep a a third more than is necessary for the preservation of good health; this lengthened slumber only serves to enervate her, makes her more delicate, and exposes her to the rebellion of the flesh; whilst sleep in moderation, accompanied by regular exercise, renders a person gay, healthy, and robust, which state undoubtedly constitutes the true perfection of the body, to say nothing of the advantages which the mind derives from it."[2]

Behold, then, my children, how many advantages of soul and body, mind, and life's duties, are herein united. By too much sleep the body becomes debilitated in place of being strengthened — that is the opinion of all physicians; whilst the mind grows stupid and heavy, and the soul weaker to resist the assaults of the senses, and all our occupations suffer immensely, because the best part of the day is lost, and a sort of general drowsiness weighs down the rest of it, even when we seem to devote it to the fulfilling of our duties. Therefore did the Wise Man say — "Love not sleep."[3] Love it not with that sensual, self-indulgent love which would make it one of life's aims.

The most formidable combat man has to fight is not always on the battle-field, but is rather that which he has to wage with his pillow. Do not let us deceive ourselves; there lies the enemy most difficult to vanquish, and the soldier who has intrepidly faced the cannon's mouth has felt his courage fail him on the Plains of Down. We must take prudent and energetic precautions against this formidable adversary. First, cultivate that firm decision of character which will listen to no wavering, and pay attention to the

---

[1] *The Laws*, 1. vii. p. 389, edit. Didot.
[2] *De l'Education des Filles*, Ch. II.
[3] Prov. 20:13.

following recommendations. If you eat too much at night there will result a long, difficult, and laborious digestion, and when you want to rise next morning you will feel as if your body were fastened to the bed; the slightest motion becomes a frightful effort, and, counselled by sloth, you find it easy to prove to yourself that it is a debt you owe your health not to torment so feeble an organization! Saint Clement of Alexandria says — "We should avoid eating too much, lest the load of food oppress us during slumber, like a heavy burden by which a swimmer is weighed down amid the waves. This practice of temperance will insure us an easy waking."[1] Why do we so often meet persons of robust health, and who enjoy the soundest slumbers, in religious communitites?[2] They eat lightly, and therefore sleep well. Do not mistake the meaning of my words. When I say they sleep well, I do not say they sleep much. They take a light repast in the evening, and then sleep that profound, tranquil sleep which many of the rich and powerful would give thousands to purchase. The repose of the just soul is calm, peaceful, and undisturbed, and his waking is fresh as the dawn of morn in the spring time. Pére Lacordaire once said to me, "You cannot imagine the comfort resulting from the short nightly rest of a religious."

The second precaution relates to the form and material of your beds. Do not choose too soft a bed; rather avoid those refinements of luxury which exhaust every ingenious contrivance to arrive at a bed of roses; such habits are so many chains holding you fast in spite of yourself, and acquiring an almost irresistible empire over your entire being. If you furnish your enemy with arms, can you wonder that he is always and easily your conqueror? The body can accustom itself to any treatment, and if we give it habits of temperance, they will prove its best, most skilful, and most economical physician. I

---

[1] *Pedag. 1.* ii. cap. ix. p. 494.
[2] "A hard couch, the chanting of Psalms at night, and the day's work, draw down slumber on that tender form." — Bossuet.

do not tell you to sleep on a board, as some religious orders do, although I have known a monk who one day made this singular avowal to me, "I could never express to you," he said, "the happiness which results from sleeping on a board; and this is really the case, for when I am away from my convent preaching, I actually cannot sleep on an ordinary bed, and have to make a sort of construction for myself which shall resemble as nearly as possible my beloved board." Despite the great happiness of sleeping on a board, I do not invite you to try it, for I fear the number and attendance of my guests would be but small. I will only say this: that the simpler and freer from luxurious contrivances your bed is, the more wholesome will be your sleep, the stronger will be your body, and, perhaps, the less exposed to danger will be your soul.

If I had not accustomed you during many years, my children, to look on religion as a friend who must not remain a stranger to anything concerning you, you might think it extraordinary that I should enter into these details. In case of need, the examples of the fathers of the Church shall be my excuse. Saint Clement of Alexandria says, "It is hurtful to the health to sleep on feathers, in which the body by its own weight sinks so deeply as to be almost entirely covered, and, so to speak, buried. The great warmth of this down rising on each side of the body stops digestion, dries up and corrupts its humors; while hard beds, which may be called nature's school for sleep, facilitate digestion, render it more wholesome and less inconvenient, and bestow on us the strength, suppleness, and activity which we require for the labors of the morrow."[1]

To these sanitary rules I will add two other counsels for promoting sleep. The Holy Ghost tells us that "Sleep is sweet to a laboring man."[2] Occupy yourself during the day, and avoid idleness. Let both soul and body have their share of that activity of movement which the Creator, Himself, has ordained for them by those laws which govern our organiza-

---

[1] *Pedag.* 1. ii. cap. ix. pp. 490, 491.
[2] Eccles. 5:11.

tion, and which we never seek to evade without suffering grave inconveniences. Let each one labor in his calling and, unless in case of sickness, he is sure to sleep soundly; and his sleep will be sweet, calm, and deep, because nature needs it to repair her lost forces. "Such is nature's law," says Galen.[1]

The Holy Ghost continues: "But the fulness of the rich will not suffer him to sleep." The last sentence specially applies, in my opinion, to the idle rich man, the man who knows not what to do with himself; and to the woman whose time is spent in hearing and repeating gossip, whose thoughts are wholly devoted to dress and worldly frivolities. Evening comes, and the poor thing is completely worn out, tired of everything, disgusted with everything, and at night carries her discontent and weariness with her to her couch. Truly in her are verified in their fullest extent the words of the Latin tragedian — "Sleep is the best part of her existence."[2] Sleep! behold what she succeeds best in! It is not much; and still it is preferable to being constantly bored, or to allowing her mind to vegetate in a deteriorating atmosphere. Unfortunately, sleep will not always come when wanted, for nature, ever provident and avenging, has made it the reward of labor.

If you wish for peaceful slumbers, keep a good conscience. "Keep the law and counsel . . . if thou sleep thou shalt not fear; thou shalt rest, and thy sleep shall be sweet."[3] Virtue thus proves itself of use everywhere; it promotes all good things, even sleep. When the conscience is not pure, when the breath of the passions is breaking into it more or less violently, the interior of the soul becomes like a stormy sea, the waves are sweeping tumultuously on to the shore, and the night's rest is destroyed by them. Once broken, restless watchfulness succeeds, and body and soul are tossed on a bed of anguish: "Even in the night he doth not rest in mind."[4] By passions, I under-

[1] Quoted by Cornelius à Lapide, *In Eccles.* v.
[2] Seneca, Hec. act. iv.
[3] Prov. 3:21, 24.
[4] Eccles. 2:23.

Fifth Discourse

stand all that disturbs the soul, that excites its emotions, and throws it off its balance; not alone those great passions which destroy soul and body; but also the minor shocks which affect the heart and intellect — self-love, vanity, jealousy, rancor, bitterness, irritability, and the daily annoyances of life. All these cares and emotions diminish sleep: " . . . the thought thereof driveth away sleep," says the Holy Ghost.[1]

The true Christian must purify his mind from all those earthly feelings; the just soul must filter away each night the dregs of the old man from his heart, keeping it pure as limpid water in which nought is found save what is clear and bright. Then will the whole being be well established in peace, and the soothing action of sleep have full power over it; for we may also say, borrowing in another sense a text of Scripture, that sound and healing slumbers are the portion of the peaceable man.[2] All the organs of the body repose in tranquillity, because there is nothing to counteract the benignant influence of night, which sheds the refreshing dews of health on the frame.

It is a common custom, my children, to wish one happy days; permit me, as the conclusion of this discourse, to wish you good and happy nights — a wish that may be always offered, even in the morning. May providence avert from you those nights which the Prophet calls "wearisome." May it grant you the peaceful and refreshing slumbers which renew life, and enable you to do more good. "Thou shalt rest, and thy sleep shall be sweet."[3]

---

[1] Ecclus. 31:1.
[2] Ecclus. 31:24.
[3] Prov. 3:24.

Sixth Discourse
A time to sleep <u>vs</u> the morning pillow...

She hath risen in the night. (Prov. 31:15)

MY CHILDREN,

Sleep has been given to man to be the support of his life, the restorer of his strength, and his best and most skilful physician, whose one sole ordinance, perfectly complied with, will often suffice for the cure of serious illnesses, or at least for the alleviation of acute pains. Sleep is the salutary bath in which life renews itself, and the whole frame regains its youth; it is an oasis in the desert of this world and when, after toilsome and weary journeys, we come therein to repose ourselves in this place of refreshment provided by Divine Providence, we often go forth again on our way in the morning with new courage and vigor. This time of sleep is needful, not alone for the body, but also for the mind; it calms agitation, it brings balm to poignant grief, it hinders precipitation in words and actions. Therefore did the ancients call night a good counselor. Even the wakefulness occasioned by passion or bodily infirmity she makes serve her own designs, for by the calm which the darkness of night spreads over everything, she recalls man to his better feelings. If he be a Christian, she touches in him the chords of prayer, and one short colloquy with God, one single glance upwards to Heaven, is sometimes enough to stifle the germs of evil, and to prepare a pure, cloudless sky for the morrow. Saint Ambrose says, "There is at times such deep and calm placidity in the just man's sleep, that it resembles an ecstasy in which, while the body reposes, the soul is, so to speak, separated from it, and united to Christ."[1] Sleep is likewise an eloquent preacher, because it reminds us of death; therefore, the ancients call it death's twin brother, and both were the children of night. The nightly approaches of sleep should make us say to ourselves — "Very soon will the other brother also come, and then I shall lie down on my couch never to rise again. This visitor of every evening should be for me a warning to prepare for that last solemn departure."

Sleep, then, is in itself most excellent; but the best things may be abused, and if we make a bad use of sleep, it will produce in us the contrary effects to those I have enumerated — that is to say, it will weaken the body, dull our ideas, and, instead of refreshing and renewing our life, it will build for us a species of living sepulcher for its entombment.

After some further details on this important point, I indicated to you the necessary physical and moral precaution for promoting the soothing and beneficial influence of the night.

It now remains for me to develop for your consideration other reflections, and these will form the subject of the present discourse.

It is not sufficient to determine the quantity of sleep, which ought to be prudently regulated, neither granting nor refusing too much to the needs of nature; we must also have regard to its quality.[2] Now according to general observation, the sleep one takes from the true evening to the true morning; that is to say, the interval between nine at night to five or six o'clock at morn — is the best, the most wholesome, and the most conducive to health. I do not mean one must necessarily sleep all the time I have mentioned, but that this is the time from which to choose one's hours of slumber. I willingly admit all the exceptions necessitated by passing events, but as a general rule, it is better to go to bed early and to rise early. Then

---

[1] *Epist. xvi.* n. iv. p. 960.
[2] The Germans have a proverb, to wit: "An hour's sleep before midnight is worth two in the morning."

is the best and most favorable time for the nocturnal bath we call sleep; the body obtains more refreshment, because the rest taken is more conformable to the laws of nature, and therefore, also it is more sweet, light, yet at the same time more profound, for it no longer partakes of that heaviness which is a sign of some abnormal state of the body. Sleep prolonged too far into the morning, because it has been too long delayed at night, has many serious disadvantages. It communicates a sickly languor to the general health; and this becomes the habitual state of some constitutions, with whom life is only a sort of perpetual convalescence, and who never attain to the enjoyment of the most precious gift of nature. Look, on the contrary, at country maidens, who are ordinarily so robust and strong; each evening they seek their beds at an early hour to repose their wearied limbs, and each morning they rise at dawn. In the winter the fire is lit early on the kitchen hearth, the housekeeping done, the business of the day arranged beforehand, the workmen's breakfasts ready to be served, all before the sun has appeared above the horizon. In summer, these same children of village life accompany the day-star in its morning course, their chest is expanded and strengthened by inhaling the fresh perfumed air which the first rays of the sun awaken, and which seems to breathe of life and health. Later on these same girls marry: they become healthy mothers of healthy children, and unless guilty of some imprudent neglect, they probably continue to lead, during many years, a life fruitful in works, and often adorned with all the freshness and charms of a vigorous old age — for their regimen is a first-rate physician, who can bestow on them a guarantee of a long life.

Whence comes it, on the other hand, that women of the world have such inherent weakness of constitution? It springs from many causes, but one of the principal is the mode of life prevalent in large towns. A portion of the night is passed in so-called evening parties, which are lengthened out into the morning; a portion of the day must then be devoted to sleep, and a general debility of constitution ensues, with weakened nerves, numbed and clogged organs, and a constant, habitual languor. Some exceptional constitutions may be strong enough to resist the strain, but it is incontestible, in the eyes of any impartial observer, that loss of health, especially among women, is in great measure due to these excesses. "Long night vigils," says a learned man, "necessarily cause a fatigue which unfavorably affects the brain and the digestive organs. Now fatigue of this kind, far from promoting slumber, renders it broken and unrefreshing. Thence results in great measure that sickly state of health we habitually observe in women who dwell in large cities; balls and parties quickly destroy their health, and these foolish and pernicious dissipations often leave their impress on their youth, but oftener still on their womanhood and old age."[1]

I foresee your objection: Then you mean to condemn evening parties? I must beg you to remark, in the first place, that if they are condemned, it is not by me, but by the facts, by nature, by the constitution of the human body. Is it true that the health of women who live much in society is frequently enfeebled? No one can deny it. Is it true that one of the principal causes of this effect is the mode in which society usually carries on its social relations? This is a fact which science every day confirms. I am far from wishing to prohibit evening parties; and perhaps you have not forgotten how some years ago, at these our monthly meetings, I endeavored to explain to you that religion is quite compatible with innocent amusement and social gatherings; on this condition, however, that they are governed by prudence and propriety, never endangering the welfare of either soul or body — for the Christian religion has so great a regard for the body, that there may well be sin in compromising health by any considerable imprudence. Cheerful evening gatherings have numerous advantages; they amuse the mind and refresh the body, they bring hearts nearer, dissipate cares, and draw closer the ties of friendship or family. Relaxation, to a certain extent, is neces-

[1] M. Desdouit's *Leçons de la Nature*, 1. iii. con. 188, t. iii. p. 125.

sary for man — that is, innocent relaxation, which does not wound virtue; and those who have any doubts on this subject should consult the writings of the greatest theologians of the Church, Saint Thomas in particular.[1] This great Doctor expresses himself on this matter with a clearness and precision, a good sense and wisdom, mingled at the same time with consideration and discretion. The rule which he lays down is, that we should take our amusements with moderation, according to time, place, and the convenience of those with whom we live. Fénelon says, "There are some people who would have you always groaning, and making yourself miserable by striving to excite in yourself a distaste for the amusements in which you are bound to partake. For my part, I must confess I cannot approve of such austerity. I prefer a more simple and natural behavior, and I believe God prefers it too. When diversions are innocent in themselves, and entered into in accordance with the usages of the position in which God has placed you, then all that is necessary is, I think, that you should take part in them with moderation and in submission to the designs of Providence. Stiff and reserved manners, wanting in complaisance and frankness, will only serve to give a false idea of piety to worldlings, who are already only too prejudiced against it, and who would imagine that the service of God demands a gloomy and melancholy life."[2]

We wish, then, that Christian society would adopt for its maxim this beautiful sentence from Saint Chrysostom — "Christians have a taste for refined pleasures, but decorum must ever preside over them."[3] It is impossible to make more reasonable concessions to human nature; and for this very reason is not religion authorized to show herself more severe towards everything which passes the bounds of prudence, propriety, or virtue, and even towards anything which might be

---

[1] *Ethics*, bk. iii. lec. 21.
[2] *Avis à une personne de la Cour, Manuel de Piété*, t. i. p. 35, edit. Dupanloup.
[3] *In Epist. ad Romanos* 24. t. 9. p. 766. Saint Chrysostom, in the same passage, recommends moderation and soberness in amusements, "Just," he says, "because I wish pleasure to be really pleasure."

injurious to our health or property? To return, then, to our subject, would it not be possible, in our family and social meetings, to combine things so as to promote the general welfare and good health of the present generation? Unless in exceptional circumstances, when one might be obliged to sit up late, would it not be possible to have parties end at an earlier hour, thus making them pleasanter, more frequent, and less injurious to health? This is the problem I wish solved; and is it not singular that it should be religion which steps in here to say to you: Have regard to your bodily interests, for it is wrong to neglect them to any great extent.

This excess in the time given to evening amusements comes to us from paganism. It existed in the days of Seneca; listen to the words in which he condemns it — "There are some people who turn night into day. . . . And, therefore, nothing can be sadder or more melancholy than the appearance of those who thus consecrate themselves, as it were, to the night. They have the complexion of sick people; they are pale and languid, and seem to bear about them flesh already dead on a living body. Even this is not the worst of the matter: their minds grow torpid, and are lost in darkness and bewildered in unrealities and clouds. How is it possible not to deplore an irregularity which causes man to abandon the light of day and pass his life in darkness."[1]

I have often asked myself: If religion imposed half the sacrifices the world demands; if it required us to spend a portion of our nights in fatiguing our minds and bodies, what would be said against it? What angry anathemas — what bitter reproaches! But as it is the world that commands, no one complains; everyone is enchanted, or at least appears to be so. Saint Francis de Sales has made some observations on this subject, where a delicate raillery peeps through deep reasoning, and I should not forgive myself were I not to quote his words to you — "We have seen nobles and their ladies pass whole nights, and even many successive nights, at play, . . .

[1] *Epist. 122.*

Sixth Discourse

yet worldlings found no fault, and friends were not uneasy; but let us make an hour's meditation, or rise a little earlier than usual to prepare for Communion, and every one runs to the physician to beseech him to cure us of the jaundice or the vapors which have seized us. We might dance during thirty consecutive nights, and nobody say a word; but after the solitary vigil of Christmas Eve, everyone is coughing and complaining all next day."[1]

The wholesome rule of "early to bed and early to rise" is most advantageous to the soul, and every occupation of life is better for it when it is followed. At night the soul feels more quiet — quiet like all things which are regular, untroubled and unperplexed by the many worries of a too worldly life. In the evening, before going to sleep, we should recollect ourselves, and examine into the day's work, with all its thoughts, desires, and actions; see what is deserving of praise or blame, and, like a careful trader, count up our gains and losses.

Think not, my children, that this practice of nightly examination belongs only to narrow-minded devotees, for it is a custom dictated by good sense and wise philosophy, as indeed are all the practices of enlightened devotion. The pagans might give a lesson on this subject to many Christians. Listen to Pythagoras — "Let not slumber seal thine eyes before thou hast examined into every action of the day. In what have I failed? What deeds have I done? What duties have I forgotten? Begin with thy first act, and go on through each one of the day. Then reproach thyself for the evil, and rejoice over the good thou hast done."[2]

"What can be more admirable," says Seneca, "than this habit of examination into every action of the day? What a peaceful slumber follows this review of our deeds! How calm it is, how deep, how full of repose, when the soul has received its award of praise or blame, after having sat in judgment on its own conduct, and submitted itself to its own jurisdiction

---

[1] *Vie dévote*, pt. 4., ch. i.
[2] *Vers dorés*, p. 40-44

and censure! For my part, I daily exert this authority over myself, and cite myself before the tribunal of my own conscience. When daylight is over, I discuss with myself the whole day; I weigh again my acts and words; I conceal nothing, I pass over nothing."[1]

Adopt this holy habit, my children; reason, piety, everything in you will be a gainer by it; a sweet serenity will overflow your soul, and you will sleep the peacefulness of angels.

You have sometimes seen children asleep. What calm! how sweet the expression of their faces! what repose of features! what grace of attitude! what perfect stillness! Let theirs be the image of your slumbers!

And now we come to the difficult point. It results from this rule of life, that you must rise early. I hear the deep sigh of dismay which rises from your affrighted couch. Well, then, let us clearly understand the meaning of these words, early rising. I am not desiring you to imitate a very delicate woman, who wrote thus during her sojourn at Vichy — "I begin my day at four o'clock in the morning, that the body may not gain too much empire over the soul!"[2] I do not propose this as your model, being well aware that, were a list opened, few would be found to inscribe themselves members of Madame Swetchine's confraternity. We will leave, then, a little undecided the meaning of the words: early rising. Let it only be as early as possible, and even then it will, perhaps, be sometimes too late. Once you have fixed your hour of rising, keep to it with the more firmness because of the difficulties to be overcome; for this troublesome couch of ours contains in the morning such an amount of magnetic fluid, that it keeps us back; I do not say against our will, but with a not unpleasing force, which seems to fasten us to the pillow. I acknowledge we are now in presence of our most terrible enemy, and our pillow is that enemy. When we would quit it in the morning, it lulls us with the artful tones of a siren, and

---

[1] *De Irâ*, 1. ii. ch. 36.
[2] *Lettres de Madame Swetchine*, t. i. p. III.

Sixth Discourse

caresses us with the utmost tenderness. It seems to say, Why leave me? Are you not well off here? What delicious warmth! What unspeakable ease! Do you not see it is still too early? Are not your limbs still fatigued because you have not rested long enough? Put your hand to your head, and you will feel that a headache is coming on, which another hour or so will take away, and then tomorrow you can get up earlier. Besides, it is so cold out of bed. What use is there in thus braving the rigor of the season? The day is long enough; you will have plenty of time for everything you want to do: Why be so uselessly hard on yourself? After this eloquent discourse, our beloved pillow extends its arms to enfold us once more, and its victory is complete. It is true the triumph was an easy one, for no one rejoices more at it than the conquered. And, accordingly, we sink back, and are buried in our bed of down for some hours longer.

I speak quite seriously, my children, when I say that one of the most difficult enemies to overcome is our morning pillow. There is but one way to secure a victory, and that is a prompt, decisive act, a military charge, a jump out of bed. Rout the enemy by a vigorous sortie, and the victory is yours. An old Capuchin once said that after many long years of religious life, his greatest cross still was having to rise at four o'clock in the morning. It is a fact, my children, there is a sacrifice to be made therein — a real, incontestable sacrifice; but, in this world, life is full of sacrifices, and each one of them is followed by a feeling of true happiness, and each victory gained gives us a wonderful and increased strength. When I meet a man who has the courage to rise at an early hour every morning, I straightway conceive a high idea of the firmness of his character, and say to myself — that man will develop an extraordinary energy, should occasions offer, for his natural strength is daily renewed in his struggle with his pillow; and this is a warfare which is often more difficult, on account of its never-ceasing recurrence, than that which the soldier wages on the battlefield.

Again, no matter how long you wait, unless, indeed, you were to remain in bed till mid-day, you will still have to make a sacrifice in leaving your pillow. Sometimes, even, the sacrifice seems greater the longer you wait, by reason of the melancholy perspective of having to get up soon; while with one moment of prompt, ready decision, the effort is made, and all the enjoyments of active life are already begun.

Lying long awake in bed has many serious disadvantages for the soul. It enervates the whole being, plunging it in a sort of effeminate, perhaps sensual, reverie, which may lead to the very brink of an abyss. Be on your guard. The butterfly fluttering gayly with brilliant wings, flies towards the flame which so treacherously lures it but to scorch it. It is the emblem of those flights of fancy in which the soul, from having approached too near deceitful lights, ends by tarnishing its pinions, and depriving them of the bloom of a pure conscience, "It is a dangerous thing," says Saint Ambrose, "when the sun comes to trouble with indiscreet rays the dreams of the sluggard on his couch."[1]

The Italian poet, speaking of morning, says, "That hour when the mind, more detached from earthly things and less clogged by the flesh, has visions almost divine."[2] Each day, after a good night's rest, we see renewed in our souls the wonders of a beautiful morning in spring. All is fresh in mind and body; our faculties are clear and bright, our life seems to feel a need of expansion — all its thoughts and ideas are tremulous with happiness, like the plants in a heavenly garden. Let the sun of prayer rise, then, on the horizon, and all germs of good will spring to life, develop themselves, and grow in proportion as the divine rays become more intense. "The manna," says the Prophet, "melted away at the rising of the sun, to show unto all, O my God, that we ought to prevent the sun to bless Thee and adore Thee at the dawning of the day, if we would

---

[1] *In Psalm cxviii.* sec. xix. n. 22, til. p. 1476.
[2] Dante, *Purgat.* ix. 16-19. Synésius calls night "something wholly divine." —*Hymn* iv. v. 6.

receive Thy precious benedictions."[1] There is one thing which ought to be remarked in the Holy Scriptures, which is that morning prayer is specially dwelt on therein. "'O Lord," says the Prophet, "in the morning thou shalt hear my voice."[2] "In the morning I will stand before thee and will see."[3] "and in the morning my prayer shall prevent Thee."[4] "We are filled in the morning with thy mercy."[5] The Lord calls Himself "the bright and morning star."[6] And Wisdom teaches, "They that watch for me early in the morning shall find me."[7] I cannot avoid seeing in these continual repetitions a fixed and firmly established principle. Between things in nature there exists natural relation ordered by divine providence, which it loves to perpetuate in the supernatural world. Now morning is the hour when life seems to recommence again on earth; it is the hour when all is born anew, when solitude seems more favorable to the first outbursts of life renewing its course, when the dews fall coolly and freshly on the plants. It is also the most propitious hour for thought — the outpouring of the dew of souls. The sky is still charged with the rain which the past night has condensed; manna is lying everywhere, but it will soon disappear, and whilst indolence is wasting its powers of mind and body in the fetters of sleep, the active soul has amassed its provision of celestial nourishment. It has formed, so to speak, the sky of its interior for the coming day, dissipating all clouds and establishing serenity till the period of its next slumbers.

One of the sweetest and most precious of the hours of life is the hour of morning prayer. I do not mean only vocal prayer by this. I mean more especially union with God by prayer, silence, and repose of the soul in God; I mean that opening of the mouth of the soul to aspire after heavenly food, and drink

---

[1] Cf. Wis. 16:20-28.
[2] Ps. 5:4.
[3] Ps. 5:5.
[4] Ps. 87:14.
[5] Ps. 89:14.
[6] Apoc. 22:16.
[7] Prov. 8:17.

in light and love, saying not a word, but hiding itself in the bosom of that best of parents we call God, and whom so few Christians really know. Ah! if you knew this gift of God — love of the early morning hours. Therein is found a freshness, a sweetness, an energy, and a peace which come direct from God. If we find ourselves on a mountain in summer at three o'clock in the morning, watching the first rays of the sun appear, the air seems to come to us more clear from not having passed through other lungs; it is the pure essence of the day-star which we breathe, and, like this, is our union with God in that hour when most men are asleep. On the divine mountains the soul obtains the first fruits of celestial favors; she is penetrated with light and love and energy, and thence results during the whole day a sweet intoxication, which, far from enfeebling the soul, gives greater firmness to our thoughts and actions, and sheds a perfume of joy over all our works. Were there no other reasons for early rising, I would still say to you: "Rise up from your pillow, because the Lord comes to visit you with His choicest favors; but the least delay will be a proof of indifference, and will force the Lord to go further, seeking a soul more worthy of His benefits. There is no one who would not each morning rise promptly if some one ran to him crying — 'Come quickly, a prince has arrived in your house, and is waiting for you.'" Put God in the prince's place, and the truth is before you.

One observation more, my children, and I have done. If you desire to accomplish anything of importance in life, rise early. In the quiet morning hours nothing comes to disturb; a calm solitude reigns around, and all business matters are more easily expedited. You may then occupy yourself with your business, or household arrangements, or with your books and intellectual pursuits if you are fond of study; the amount of work thus done will in a few years be incalculable.

By rising two hours earlier every day, you will have gained at the end of forty years more than twenty-nine thousand hours — that is to say, more than seven years, counting only

Sixth Discourse

the twelve hours of the day in which man works. To have augmented one's life by seven years in forty is an immense thing, and all that may be done by steady application during that time is almost incredible. Saint Clement of Alexandria says, "We must snatch from sleep as much of our life as is possible."[1] Sleep is indeed a thief who steals from us our most precious possession; a robber whom we cannot wholly escape, but from whom we may wrest much ground, and whom we may prevent encroaching too much. "We scarcely live one half our lives," said the Elder Pliny; the other half is spent in a state resembling death. . . . And besides that, we should not count the days of childhood, when we know nothing, nor those of old age, when we only exist to suffer."[2] Let us then have the courage to take away each day somewhat from this twin-brother of death, who thus divides our life in two, reserving the better part for himself. Let us give to nature what is necessary for her, but let us make no concession to indolence.

The most favorable time for this pillage is the early morning. "The very quality of time is different at that hour," says Madame Swetchine.[3] One hour in the morning is worth two in the evening, because the mind is clearer, and more recollected; its powers are not yet spent, nor has it been exhausted by the fatigues of the day. The morning hours resemble in their activity of mind and renewed vigor of soul the first hour's work of a horse just harnessed to a carriage. Therefore, this same writer, whom I love to quote, recommends early rising, "in order to keep for one's self at any cost some hours of solitude and liberty during the early morning time." "It was not only," says one of her friends, "in order to consecrate to God the first hours of the day that she began it so early, but also that she might always have a considerable portion of time for study." She told me, on the same day, that the pleasure she took in it increased with years. "The pleasure I feel," she

---

[1] *Pedag. l.* ii. cap. ix. p. 497.
[2] *Pedag. l.* vii. cap. li. al. l.
[3] *Lettres*, t. ii. p. 442.

added, "is so intense, that when I approach my work-table to pursue my cherished occupations, my heart beats from very gladness."[1] She elsewhere declares, "That if these morning hours were lost, all the rest of the day was also lost to her."[2] If you, my children, wish in like manner not to be deprived of leisure, rise early. Then you will be able to do all you wish: no one comes to interrupt, and you are able to devote your inmost powers to the serious and real duties of your existence; and when the hour of pillage arrives, that is to say, the hour when your life must be cut up into little bits and wasted on innumerable trifles, more or less necessary, you will at least have first secured the best and most valuable portion of it. If you get up late, your life will be a constant spoil for any one who wants to have a shred of it. Plato says somewhere (and you will scarcely think the morality of a pagan writer to be too severe) — "It is a disgrace to the mistress of a house to have herself awaked by her servants, in place of being the first to awake them."[3] This may seem a rather exaggerated notion, yet if these things could be thus arranged, would not everything go on better in the interior of families? The wife, as we have said in the words of the Holy Ghost, is the sun of her household, and it is the sun who everywhere announces the waking hour in the universe. It rises on the horizon, and at once all nature awakes: plants, animals, and man. The sun does not wait to be roused by his satellites; he himself gives the signal. Let it be thus also with the valiant woman: "As the sun when it riseth to the world in the high places of God, so is the beauty of a good wife for the ornament of her house."[4]

---

[1] *Lettres*, t. ii. P. 443.
[2] *Ibid*, p. 126.
[3] *The Laws*, l. vii. p. 389, edit. Didot. "Demosthenes was quite out of humor, if it happened that any artisan began his work earlier than he did." — Cicero, *Tuscul.* l. iv. cap. xix.
[4] Ecclus. 26:21.

Seventh Discourse
The Valiant Woman is the "sun" of her household, giving light and warmth.

She hath given a prey to her household, and victuals to her maidens.
(Prov. 31:15)

MY CHILDREN,
We have now finished the very ordinary, yet very important, question of sleep. It is a blessing sent us daily by Divine Providence to restore our strength, renew our life, and give time to the counsels of wisdom to prevail over the weakness and precipitation of man. Sleep is a precious balm, an invigorating bath to soul and body, a prudent counsellor, and a daily sermon to remind us of our approaching and final departure. But like every good thing, sleep is subject to abuses, and then it produces effects which are quite contrary to those which were intended by the Creator: it weakens; it stupefies; it numbs all our powers, and becomes a living sepulchre for humanity. If these abuses have reference to its quality, that is to say, if the hours ordained by nature be considerably altered, if night be turned into day and day into night, they become a sure means of ruining the constitution, and of preparing for the time of old age, years of constant ailing and half convalescence never perfected into health. Balls and late hours have killed more women than the most austere mortifications have

The Valiant Woman

done; and if religion required the sacrifices which are imposed by the world on its followers, there never could be enough reproaches heaped on it. From both a moral and physical point of view, it is better to go early to bed and rise early. Everything profits by it: health, business, the excellence and efficacy of prayer. But I must not conceal from you that the warfare with one's pillow is, from its very sweetness, one of the most difficult, one of the most trying to man's courage; and to break each morning the fetters of bed, it is necessary to display the utmost firmness and energy. This enemy is all the more dangerous from its caresses. Its allurements are the more treacherous, because, being so full of charms, we end by allowing ourselves to be persuaded — by believing that our adversary is in the right, and that, after all, it is cruel to make such martyrs of ourselves. I do not think, my children, I have concealed any of the difficulties; but I have pleaded my cause before the bar of your own good sense and wisdom, and I think I have won at that tribunal; yet, should you decide on appealing against the sentence, and have the case called on anew before the tribunal of sloth; should you listen to its numerous advocates; I am certain beforehand that the first judgment will be reversed. Be it so, I am content to lose on the following condition: that this explanation shall be inserted into the sentence — This cause was gained at the bar of reason; but in the supreme court of indolence, sloth, surrounded by its advocates, procured the reversal of the first judgment.

The remainder of the text may be thus translated, "The valiant woman . . . hath given a prey to her household, and victuals to her maidens."

Formerly, my children, when society and families were imbued with Christianity, the domestics, according to the etymology of the word, were looked on as really part of the household, for *domestic* is derived from the Latin word *domus*, signifying a house. In those times a family formed but one body; the father and mother were its head, and the domestics had their place in its organization; they were only secondary members, it is true, but still they belonged to the body; and therefore they always remained in the same family. Their whole life was spent in it, and when they could no longer work, they were cared for with paternal, or, sometimes, filial affection; and when the hour of death arrived, they dropped off from sheer old age, as a branch dies on the trunk. Feelings of kindliness and Christian charity united masters to their servants; the latter, as was right, kept in their own station, but they felt themselves cherished; they loved in their turn, and no links of massive gold can bind like the tie of love. Saint Augustine speaks with tenderness of an old nurse who had watched over the childhood of his mother, and had even carried about on her back Saint Monica's father, as young girls are wont to carry little children.[1] "These recollections," continues Saint Augustine, "her advanced years, and her excellent conduct, assured her in a Christian household the respect of her masters, who had committed to her charge the bringing up of their daughters. Their confidence was justified by her zeal; for, when necessary, she could be conscientiously strict in correcting them, and admirably prudent in instructing them."

In the present day things are much altered, and such examples are very rare. Undoubtedly, there are some praiseworthy exceptions, and servants are still to be found who are attached to their masters, who form part of the family, and who are treated as children of the house. Service is easy and pleasant to them, because it is chiefly dictated by affection. They bear patiently with the defects of their masters; their masters, in their turn, bear with the defects of their servants; and so everything goes on with that relative perfection, which, though sometimes very imperfect, yet after all is often the least evil, and the only possible good, in the affairs of this life. Yes, we still meet Christian families where service is thus understood and practiced; but, alas! They become rarer every day. Nowadays, thanks to the spirit of pride, independence, and irreligion everywhere prevalent, good servants are very difficult to find,

---

[1] *Confessions*, l. ix. cap. viii.

and perhaps good masters, too; for as two fires brought in contact mutually inflame each other, so one may say the bad qualities of the servants increase those of the masters, and *vice versa*. Servants have most exaggerated pretensions; they cannot bear the slightest observation; everything wounds them: while, on the other hand, masters do not always command in a Christian-like manner. And so one hears nothing but a universal concert of complaints and recriminations: masters finding fault with their servants, servants disparaging their masters, until some houses become like omnibuses, where servants enter only to leave again immediately.

I have sometimes said to you, my children, that were I preaching to your husbands, I could add a sort of counterpart, which would not be the contrary, but the complement of these instructions; but that as I am addressing you, my words must be limited to your duties. I must now say that were I preaching to your servants, I would have many counsels to give them, which would be of much utility in the organization of your households; but they are not here, and it is you whom I have to instruct, therefore I leave in the shade all that concerns the obligations of servants.

It appears to me that you will be sure to fulfil your duties towards them well, if you enter into the spirit of this verse — "She hath risen in the night; she hath distributed work and food to her domestics." See the sun; it rises on the horizon, and in pouring forth its beams, it seems at the same time to distribute work to every creature, and in recompense to prepare beforehand the supplies necessary for his sustenance. Is it not the sun who, by giving light to the world, invites the artisan to re-enter his stall, the laborer to return to the field, and the sailor to leave the port? Is it not he who prepares and vivifies the seed in the earth's bosom, fertilizing and bringing it to that point of maturity which the statesman as well as the peasant is impatiently awaiting. A woman, says the Scripture, should be the sun of the household. She should dispense light and warmth as the day-star does. She gives light when she

Seventh Discourse

assigns to each one his share in the labors of the day, apportioning the work of the house, and dividing it into wise and equitable portions. Having thus regulated matters in the morning, she superintends their execution afterwards. Then all goes on admirably, for it is directed by the orderly spirit of the mistress of the house. Her glance, which takes in everything, diffuses light around, and this light is the most forcible and persuasive of counselors, and at the same time the gentlest yet strictest of monitors. A woman who presides over her household affairs has no need of talking much; her presence speaks for her, and the mere knowledge that she keeps her eyes open, and notices the smallest details, causes all to move on smoothly as on a railroad. On the other hand, contemplate the house whose mistress rises very late, and is mentally asleep for the rest of the day. There everything is left to chance; confusion reigns in minds and business. It is a perfect pell-mell of ideas and objects — a disorder which recalls the primitive chaos. Madame sleeps all the morning; the domestics do pretty much the same thing. She dreams all day, occupying herself only with dress, gossip, and visits, while her household is left to take care of itself, the children are neglected, and business is left to accumulate in frightful disorder.

A woman, being the sun of her household, must not content herself with giving light only; she should give warmth also, because the light should proceed from her heart. You are bound, my children, to watch over your domestics; to take note of their proceedings in your house and out of it, and most particularly to observe them in their intercourse with your children, for very often both the soul and body of a child has been destroyed by servants. And could I be permitted to reveal all that the history of the human heart teaches in this respect, I could tell the most fearful tales.

I had the charge of a school for very young boys some twenty years ago, when one day I received a note from a highly indignant parent, who told me bitterly that his child had become corrupted in our school. I knew the contrary, but

The Valiant Woman

could not say so, and as often happens in such circumstances, had to bear silently the unmerited reproach. Some time after I got permission to speak, and it was then very easy for me to prove to the father that his son had been perverted by associating with a servant in his own house.

Guard your children, then, by closely watching your domestics. Acquaint yourself with their goings out and their comings in, their behavior and the society they frequent; pay heed to their words and actions. But I conjure you, let all this be kindly done; let your watchfulness be tempered by the warmth of brotherly love. Entertain a regard for your servants, remembering that they are of the same human nature as yourselves, and have been made after the image of God, and redeemed by the blood of Christ. As much as is possible, speak gently to them; and should a sally of impatience escape you, seek an opportunity of repairing it by an act of kindness. Let your watchfulness be neither fidgety nor suspicious; never be a spy on their actions — for one often makes men good by believing them to be so, or bad by manifesting a contrary impression at all events, you wound their feelings, and, perhaps, irremediably. Avoid all tendency to ill-humor, peevishness, or caprice. Today the mistress is in good humor, so all will be right; the servants may amuse themselves, and commit any folly they like, quite sure of its being passed over in silence. Next day the moon is in a bad quarter, and evil is the fate of every inmate and of every servant of the house. Madame's coffee is cold, although it is as hot as usual; the soup is too salty, though flavored as on every other day. The room is smoking, and it is the servant's fault, though the poor man made neither the wind nor the chimney. Then comes a commotion enough to frighten any one, and the mistress' voice — or rather, her screaming — resounds from cellar to attic, from the yard to the neighboring houses. Nothing lessens the prestige of authority like such conduct; servants grow weary, their patience becomes exhausted, they lose all feelings of confidence and affection, because they see that no regard is felt for

Seventh Discourse

them, that they are treated as if they were inferior creatures, without respect or consideration; and even on those days when whims are not in the ascendant, it is only a change to haughty airs and a disdainful silence.

Undoubtedly, my children, there is a medium to be observed in all this; servants are often unreasonable, and abuse the kindness shown them; they are, or may be, exacting and indiscreet; they want to have their masters faultless, while they are blind to their own shortcomings. An ancient philosopher says: "Treat them as friends and they become insubordinate; keep them at a distance and they conceive hatred and resentment for you."[1] The middle course of prudence is difficult to find; but this same difficulty of finding a wise medium exists in all the affairs of this world, and must be overcome, notwithstanding its perplexities. The heart of a Christian woman appears to be marvelously fit for this work of conciliation, for she will know how to preserve her authority and display a steady firmness on necessary occasions, remembering Fénelon's words: "The less reasonable people are, the more necessary is it that they should be restrained by fear."[2] The valiant woman will therefore be able to hold her own against those carping, pretentious beings, who make themselves simply ridiculous by their requirements, and will know how to keep them in their proper place when wisdom demands it. But in her ordinary conduct she will always remember that those under her control are her brethren in Jesus Christ, that kindness and gentleness are the most Christian-like modes of persuasion, and that severity should only be employed in cases where good sense and forbearance have proved insufficient.

Fénelon also says that in some houses the domestics are looked on "almost in the light of horses, and as if they were of a different nature, and only created for the convenience of their masters."[3] Nothing can be more opposed to the precepts

---

[1] Confucius, *Entr. Philos.* ch. 17.
[2] *De l'Education des Filles*, ch. 7.
[3] *Ibid.*

The Valiant Woman

of faith and reason: Your servants are your brethren, and should be cherished and treated as such; they owe you service and fidelity; if they fail in these, recall them to their duty, but do so, as far as is possible, with a charitable compassion and firmness not unmixed with affection. One single kind word said from the heart is often enough to disperse clouds, dissipate prejudices, and lay the foundation of a real and sincere affection for you in the hearts of your domestics; and is not that far preferable to those forced relations, that cold, stiff intercourse which chills hearts and embitters life far more than we are willing to believe? We have a fable in proof of this truth — the ant's friendship was not to be disdained.

The valiant woman hath distributed food and work to her domestics. The Holy Spirit neglects no details, because everything in life is of importance. Make your servants do their work, for it is quite right to do so, but do not grudge them proper nourishment and care. Treat them as if they were really children of the house: Christian charity is not the only thing concerned in acting thus; your own service will likewise be a gainer. Do not weigh with a niggardly hand what may tend to their well-being and the alleviation of their state. You will gain in one way what you lose in another; besides, is not a little true affection from a devoted heart of more worth than a piece of gold?

Neither is it only food and material assistance which you are bound to give your servants. How I love to see a Christian woman enlarge her maternal heart to find place therein not only for her children, but for all the inmates of her house. Yes, she ought to have the affection of a mother for all, so that even the lowest may feel that they too have a share in the kind, warm sentiments of her heart. Then will she truly realize the comparison I love to repeat incessantly, because it is so admirably true in its grand simplicity, and because, as often as I examine it, I discover therein new beauties; then will the valiant woman be the sun of her household. The day-star sheds its light over the clouds, the lofty mountains, and gilded palaces, but it does not neglect the lowly flower of the valley, and the smallest blade of grass participates in its light and heat. Its beams may not fall on it in such abundance as on the oaks of the forest, but the light is still the same, and the portion it does receive is sufficient for its life and gladness. Thus does the valiant woman lavish her inmost affections on her family and true friends, but reserves still a share for her domestics; and though she gives to them less than to her husband and children, yet it is derived from the same source, and has often the same value for them.

And after this labor, care, and affection, you must not expect your domestics to be faultless. To your servants I would say, bear with the defects of your masters and mistresses, for the very best must have faults, and the surest way for you to lessen their effect is to meet them with patience and unfailing docility; meekness and patience will do far more than anger and violent recrimination, as wool is the substance which the soonest arrests the impetuous course of a cannon-ball. To you, my children, I say, bear with the defects of your servants, for all will have them. With these two safeguards — with a certainty of patience and forbearance on the part of masters and on that of servants — we should soon introduce peace into the interior of families. Should the curb of forbearance give way on one side, it would still hold on the other; such is the admirable teaching of Christianity, which, wherever there exists a connection between men, has established reciprocal duties on such a firm, solid basis, that should one side fail, the other must become only the more strong to resist. Thus, to husbands it inculcates love and respect; to wives, love, respect, and submission; to masters, kindness; to servants, deference and patience; all this in such sort that should one side prove faithless to their obligations, the fidelity of the other to theirs ought only to augment. Nature evidently would speak another language. If our neighbor be wanting to his duty, we hold ourselves freed from ours; and this spirit of barter in regard to wrong-doing is, perhaps, not one of the least causes of the disturbances which afflict families and society.

There are some faults which, as Fénelon remarks, have penetrated into the very marrow of our bones. "Therefore," says the Archbishop of Cambray, "if you try to correct them in your servant, it is not he who errs in not being corrected, but you who are wrong in undertaking to correct him."[1] You have a horse blind of an eye; you insist on his seeing clearly with both eyes! Why, it is really you who are altogether blind. Alas my children, we are all of us a little blind, and we must bear one another's burdens. You have a servant who is not possessed of the requisite judgment; why, then, do you employ him in difficult matters? He has made a blunder, but were not you the real cause of it? You have another who cannot see many yards before him; it is not his fault — he is short-sighted. You become irritated because he cannot distinguish an object half a mile off; it is you who are unreasonable. Another is lame, and you would have him walk without halting. Can you not see you are requiring an impossibility? What I mean is, my children, that our poor human nature is full of moral infirmities, and that when we once find some such failing forming part of our neighbor's character, we must make allowance for it, and not require a reformation in what cannot be altered. "Bear ye one another's burdens,. . . ."[2] says Saint Paul, and herein is contained wisdom's precept for peace and domestic happiness. But perhaps you will say — "She has no brains; I can get no good of her." Alas! a want of brains, at least in some phases of the moon, is to be everywhere met with. Have you not yourself sometimes had those attacks of mental brain fever? Have indulgence, then, for others. Besides, you should not be so difficult to please in servants, or you will end by getting none at all. Be on your guard against that notion of something better; it often causes the loss of what is really good. You have a servant who, you declare, is under the moon's influence,

[1] *Lettres Spirituelles*, 193, t. i. p. 554, edit. Didot
[2] Gal. 6:2.

Seventh Discourse

for she too, like the Queen of Night, has her horns or sharp angles now on one side, now on the other. You must change. Very well, do so; and the next you take, in place of having two horns, will have four. The only difference is that they will perhaps be found on another side; instead of the right, they will be on the left. Your present maid is sulky: the next will be passionate. You had one who always argued: you will get another who will be whimsical. Choose between them. Believe me, it is better to bear the evil you know, unless it become wholly intolerable. This world and all in it is full of miseries; make the best of them — grumbling and changing will not help you.

"This is all very well," some of you tell me. "But what you say applies to those who have a large establishment, and, with my modest means, the most I can afford is a nursery-maid and cook." In such a case, if you will allow me, I will find you a family to govern, whose members are numerous and insubordinate. The Fathers of the Church teach us that the mind of man is so organized as to constitute a household in itself, in which no one is wanting, not even the porter. There is the understanding, the soul properly so called, the imagination, and the senses. Saint Augustine says, "We may look on the understanding as the husband; the soul as the wife."[1] I would add, that the imagination, with its many caprices, represents a troop of disorderly domestics, and the five senses are the five porters keeping the doors opening on the streets.[2] To make all these agree with each other and work together is not easy! When the understanding desires one thing, the heart wishes for another; it is husband and wife on the point of quarrelling. Then comes the imagination with its visions, its chimerical ideas, its fantastic racket by day and night. Is not this a household excellently well fitted to exercise your patience? And the porters at the gates — the eyes, the ears, without counting the whole legions of busy nerves that cause more worry than all besides. What a household! What confusion! What a Tower of

---

[1] *De Cen. cont. Man.* l. ii. n. 15, t. i. p. 1086.
[2] *Januis sensum*, says Saint Augustine, *De Gen. ad Litter.* l. xii. n. 43, t. iii. p. 496.

Babel! Here I will repeat to you, my children, the words of Scripture: Rise before day to give food and work to this household; that is, bring them into order from the dawn of day. Clear out your imagination, which will perhaps take more time and trouble than the arranging of dishevelled locks! See how scattered and wandering are your ideas, how this foolish imagination sings and chatters saucily, how she argues, how she rages, in a word, how absurd she is! The understanding endeavors to bring her to reason. It is useless! It is labor lost! she only screams the more, and is just as unreasonable, but more obstinately violent than before. She makes such a noise, that, as Saint Gregory remarks, "It might be the multiplied voices of many women with freshly sharpened tongues."[1]

Here is a promising household to reduce to order each morning! You complain of having nothing to do: I will find you plenty. Pacify all this uproar, introduce harmony into all this confusion, and so act that this harmony shall not be essentially disturbed all day, and then I promise you a certificate as an excellent mistress of a house. Formerly, all this commotion did not exist in man's poor head, and wherefore? Because it was devoted to God, and then all man's powers, his mind, heart, will, imagination, and senses, were in subjection to the head of the house, because that head himself was obedient to God. Since the first revolt, all has been set wrong in man, and our poor human nature resembles a household where all are wrangling: husband, wife, and servants — that is to say, mind, heart, and imagination. There is a very simple means of restoring peace, not entirely, but still very tolerably for this world; restore God to His rightful place in the household, let Him be its head and its governor, let the thought of Him be the motive power, and all will soon be in order. I know of nothing more efficacious, especially in the morning, for the purification of our interior and the establishing of calm in our whole being, than a glance towards heaven, a thought of love directed on high which brings back to us in its descent the peace of God!

[1] *Moral*, l. i. cap. xxx. t. i. p. 546, edit. Migné.

Seventh Discourse

In the early morning, when the head is aching, lay it at the foot of the Cross; when the heart is suffering, lay it on the heart of our Saviour; when the imagination is feverish and excited, calm it with a drop of the precious blood of Jesus Christ; when the whole being is in ebullition, cool it refreshingly by asking of God to let fall upon you the precious dew of heaven.

Be faithful to these recommendations, my children, and you will repose during the day in the shade of your vine and fig-tree — that is to say, you will enjoy that interior happiness which God has promised to those He loves, and which is one of the sweetest rewards of virtue: "And every man sat under his vine and under his fig-tree: and there was none to make them afraid."

---

[1] 1 Mach. xiv. 12.

EIGHTH DISCOURSE
The Valiant Woman considers the "good things" for her children, and is always the first to rise.

She hath considered a field, and bought it: with the fruit of her hands she hath planted a vineyard. (Prov. 31:16)

MY CHILDREN,
"The valiant woman hath risen in the night, and hath distributed food and labor to her maidens." The superintendence of her domestics is one of her principal occupations, and that this superintendence may be conscientiously and actively performed, she begins it with the early morning: She is the first up, or at least one of the first, in the house, and her example proves the best sermon and most efficacious counsel. Like the star of the day, she gives the signal for her household to recommence their labors; her presence infuses warmth into the most indifferent, and animates the most apathetic; none can wholly withstand her influence — "... And there is no one can hide himself from his heat."[1] This domestic superintendence must be directed by reason, prudence, and real esteem; for the valiant woman will remember that her servants are of the same nature as herself, that they are her brethren in Jesus Christ, and that they are entitled to be treated with consideration in their quality of men and Christians. She makes but one family of her entire household, whose members, though placed on

[1] Psalm 18:7.

different rungs of the social ladder, yet all participate in the common life. Every one stays in his own place, and it is this diversity in the hierarchy which causes order and beauty. But as the plants in a garden, though all inhaling the same sunshine and air, yet receive each a different share of nature's bounty, so in the garden of the family each one has his special portion, more or less abundant, of dew and heat. First the stately trees, then the shrubs, and last of all the little flowers that grow at their feet.

We also found, taking the words of our text in another sense, and following an idea familiar to the fathers, that the human soul, with the understanding, the heart, the imagination, the senses, and the nerves represent a complete household where each faculty plays its part of father, mother, children, servants, and porters, and that it was no slight difficulty to know how to maintain in peace all the numerous members of this same human family called *I*.

Let us today explain this verse — "She hath considered a field, and bought it: with the fruit of her hands she hath planted a vineyard." The sacred writings first depicted for us the valiant woman actively employed in the interior of her house. She is the joy and consolation of her husband, and in her loving heart he finds a source of good, and treasures of peace and confidence. She has spun wool and flax; she watches over the labors of her household; she rises before the day, and whilst nature is still slumbering, she distributes food and work to her domestics.

The Holy Ghost next proceeds to describe the activity of the valiant woman with regard to external matters. "She hath considered a field, and bought it: with the fruit of her hands she hath planted a vineyard." Corn and wine are the two great sustaining powers of human life; amidst all earth's productions there are none so universally used or so indispensable; therefore, does the Scripture employ them by preference to represent agricultural riches. In these matters the woman's wishes should be subordinate to her husband's; and though she may seek to influ-

Eighth Discourse

ence him by her advice, suggestions, and entreaties, the final decision should come from the head of the house. Therefore, you must always bear in mind in what is to follow, that the wife is acting in concert with her husband, and that everything is decided by mutual agreement.

"She hath considered a field." She should in effect be ever mindful of all that regards the prosperity of her family. "She hath considered," *Consideravit.* She must do nothing hastily, she must deliberate seriously; for there is property whose acquisition is only a burden, and there is property which brings an increase of wealth and pleasure. She should buy nothing without having the means of paying for it; one of the greatest evils of our time is the habit of exceeding the limits of our means in the purchases we make. As soon as a little plot of ground is seen to be for sale, it is greedily coveted; the purse is empty, but that does not matter; it is bought, to be paid for somehow in the future. This ambition, which is to be met with in a greater or less degree according to each one's social condition, is one of the principal causes of the suffering and want of the present day. In business, in commerce, in agriculture, inconsiderate expenses and speculations are entered into, until the wealth of many persons is merely fictitious; there is a splendid front to the mansion, yet it conceals nothing but ruins behind; and the lives of many gentlemen and merchants who have large estates are passed in tortures, like those of a man who is condemned to be always wearing garments which are too small for him. These garments are an image of a relatively moderate income combined with immoderate desires. In such a state all is hollow, the whole foundation is emptiness and falsehood, and inevitable ruin is the consequence. Let the valiant woman be alive to this danger; let her beware of what shines too brightly and promises too much; let her buy fields and plant vineyards, but only after having well considered everything, and examined into the state of the property to be purchased, and also into that of her own purse. It is far more conducive to happiness and peace in families to have a moderate fortune with contentment of heart and an assured future. Happiness does not depend on externals, but on the manner in which we know how to enjoy them, and so to derive more or less pleasure from them. The poor man, who can only just earn his daily bread, is happier than the rich one, whose life is but one continual anxiety and ever-consuming fever which haunts even his troubled slumbers.

The text of Scripture which we are commenting on teaches us that fathers and mothers of families may, and ought to, occupy themselves about the prudent increase of their means in order to provide for their children's future; it is a serious obligation which religion, good sense, and parental love imposes on them. They ought to endeavor daily by a wise foresight, and by all honest, legitimate means to augment their patrimony, to lay by something that they may leave their children suitably provided for. To act otherwise would be to forget the most sacred laws, and to imitate the unnatural conduct of those parents who take extravagance and selfishness as their only guides, and with whom all goes right if they can enjoy themselves unrestrainedly, and nothing occurs to give them any cause of uneasiness.

Religion does not content itself with sanctioning the precepts of the law of nature; she lays down rules for their proper and wise observance. She orders a father and mother to attend to the amelioration of their fortune, but always with the condition that the poor shall not be forgotten; and very often what is snatched from a strict economy to be poured into the lap of the poor brings in happiness and blessings, even temporal ones, more than the most skilful calculations could produce. Religion permits the increasing of our capital and revenues, but on the condition that there should be no infringement of the laws of honor and honesty; that there should be no skillfully colored frauds, none of those cunning tricks which merit a name I would not dare to pronounce here; none of those ingeniously perfidious precautions, which, for our poorer neighbors, are no better than snares which are spread in the coverts for the innocent creatures of wood and field. No; religion can never sanction fortunes so acquired. They are marked with the brand of injustice and iniquity; they bear upon them the ineffaceable stain of a sinful origin. This wickedness is the very source of rivalries and quarrels in families, and it is the Providence of God it should be so. Bad seed was sown in the commencement, and this seed has developed hidden tares, which will always overrun the field of such families. I am very fond of proverbs, because they are the result of long and profound experience, the coin as it were of the nation's wisdom, and one has just occurred to me which applies to my subject — "Ill-gotten goods never prosper." No, they never prosper, although outwardly things may appear successful; they never prosper, because the events of life, which are God's messengers, annihilate those sinfully gathered fortunes, just as the passer-by sweeps down a house of cards; they never prosper, because even in the case of continued, ever-increasing prosperity, the justice of God still finds the means of making the possessors unhappy in the midst of every external enjoyment; and, by some unknown power of metamorphosis, all those things which ought to be for them a cause of joy, become on the contrary drops of gall. There are sicknesses in which the most exquisite wine tastes like sour vinegar; and there are also moral illnesses, inexpressible disgusts, whose cause is unknown. It is the justice of God which inflicts them in certain circumstances, and then the very quality of objects and their action on the soul seem to change their nature: roses are transformed into thorns, and the finest liquors into bitter draughts. In one of our future conferences we will return to this subject, and detail it at greater length.

"The valiant woman has planted a vineyard with the fruit of her hands." I do not desire, my children, to make you follow the plough, or send you to weed in the vineyards, but should you possess a country seat, or should one of your friends have one, I would advise you to go there from time to time at least, and breathe that pure, fresh air, which gives health and wisdom. Living for a while in the country has ineffable advantages. It gives us relaxation from our toils, it calms both brain and imagination, it breaks through the routine of that artificial existence so often led in towns, it restores us to ourselves and to tranquillity of mind. There is more practical instruction than I can tell you to be gathered in the fields. The Scripture tells us that the wisdom of God is seen in the works of His hands. Every creature has something to teach us after its own manner — the ant, the bird of the air, the flower of the field. A kind of relationship of mind and true affection establishes itself between us and the objects surrounding us; order, wisdom, life, and tranquil happiness reign everywhere, and all these precious gifts are reflected back upon our inmost being. Yes, go often into the country, and if you possess the peace and confidence of a just soul, the scenes of nature will augment that moral well-being; for the creation is a mirror reflecting a part of the grandeur and beauty of the Divine Essence, at the same time that by its silent calm it is an image of the eternal peace of God. If you cannot plant vines yourself, go see them planted, and you will yourself learn how the soil is hollowed out, the young plant pressed down and covered up with earth. You will see the sprouting of the young shoots; you will become aware of the injury the frosts may work, and of the rich harvest which the combined powers of light, heat, and rain are preparing.

You must then enter into yourself and say — My heart is the vineyard of our heavenly Father: I, too, should daily plant therein a vine of good sort; sink it deeply into the earth, that is, into the inmost recesses of my own heart, cover it with the precautions of Christian prudence, guard it from cold, and keep it always exposed to the rays of the sun, and to the beneficent action of the dews of heaven. Go likewise into the fields, and when you behold the harvest ripening with the golden hues of autumn, say to yourself — When will the fruits of my heart be ripe for the harvest? O my God I vouchsafe that I too may bring forth good grain to be changed into Your substance.

Eighth Discourse

I hear you tell me that neither you nor your friends possess a place in the country. Well, but have you not a garden, or at all events some tiny spot where flowers may grow? For I desire most earnestly to find some means of applying to your life the text of Scripture I am at present expounding. If you cannot plant vines, at least sow flower seeds. If you can do no more, do at least as prisoners have done, give them a shelter on your window-sill — get a little earth and sow flower seeds. A flower has something of life, of freshness, and of beauty, which makes it a companion, and speaks to us in a divine language. A flower! It is the image of a thought from God, as a verse is the image of a poet's thought. A flower seems to look at us, and its look is the opening of its corolla. A flower has life, and a most graceful life; a life which is the symbol of candor, innocence, and modesty. The expanding of a flower under the first rays of the sun teaches us sweetly that there is another Sun whose light should expand our hearts. From the flowers that love to grow under the shelter, we learn lessons of humility and a hidden life; and when by their flagging and drooping heads they seem to ask for water to renew their dried-up life, they teach us to solicit also the true dew of souls. Finally, when they fade and fall, they give us a signal, and remind us how our lives too will soon pass away, and that the existence of flowers and man, though apparently so different in duration, are equal in eternity, where a thousand years are but as one day. Therefore, my children, I beseech you to cultivate flowers, for the contemplation of that charming portion of creation calms, softens, and soothes; it refreshes the eye and strengthens the heart; for so does it ever come to pass that all that is fresh, blooming, and full of life, exercises a happy influence over us, and causes all the powers of our mind to expand.

"The valiant woman hath considered a field, and bought it: with the fruit of her hands she hath planted a vineyard." We may also believe that under the designation of bread and wine, the

Holy Scripture intended to include all the good things of our temporal life. The valiant woman ought to direct her attention to all points; to everything that may be useful to her husband, children, and domestics; she ought to endeavor to further their interests by following those rules of prudence, probity, honor, and moderation, of which we have already spoken. Woman often possesses more intelligence for little details than man; she has a finer perception of a multitude of things which wholly escape him; her part is to foresee, to find out, to calculate beforehand, to submit her ideas to her husband, and act in concert with him. I do not assuredly wish to excite an ill regulated ambition in the mind of a mother of a family, but I am most anxious to explain to you all your duties, and even all that may legitimately be permitted to you; and thus I would answer beforehand those persons who reproach Christianity with seeking to make of a married woman a kind of nun, occupying herself exclusively with religious confraternities and practices of devotion. A truly pious woman will, while keeping faithful to all that is enjoined by an enlightened piety, neglect nothing which has regard to even the temporal prosperity of her family; and should she seek to imitate the life and religious practices of a nun, "such a devotion," says Saint Francis de Sales, "would be extravagant, misplaced, and unbearable."[1] On the other hand, let us avoid the excesses of an ungoverned ambition, for ambition is a passion which soon runs off the rails of good sense and Christian prudence. I would have that amount of steam which makes everything move along in order and safety. A deficiency of steam means torpor and death, while the excess which causes us to run off the line is another and no less serious inconvenience. Neither of these extremes can satisfy. And what I desire to see in the interior of homes is well-regulated steam; that is to say, the agency of a thoughtful woman, free from inordinate anxiety, but seriously devoting herself in all honor and uprightness to the interests of her household; an active but well-balanced mind, economical without parsimony, orderly without affectation, and while

---

[1] *Introduction to the Devout Life*, pt. i. ch. iii.

wisely doing the honors of her house, forgetting neither the interests of her children nor her duties as the mother of a family.

Let us raise our thoughts still higher. Holy Scripture has usually a hidden meaning under the letter of its words, to direct us to a better world. We will strip off that outer husk of the literal meaning, and say that bread and wine signify not only all that is best and most useful to man in material things, but that they also symbolize all that is good and advantageous in spiritual matters. The valiant woman should, therefore, lay up in her heart a constant provision of good things, in order to be able when occasion offers to distribute them to her family. In the society she frequents she must know how to collect stores of helpful sayings and valuable hints; she must then ponder them well. "She hath considered." It is not safe to pick everything that grows in the garden of this world, for the earth often produces more poisonous than wholesome or sweet smelling plants. The duty of a mother of a family is to make a sensible and religious choice, and put aside all that might injure the faith or tarnish the purity of her children's minds. "She hath considered." Before taking her children into the world, she considers whether the moment is propitious; whether their minds are not yet too unformed, too accessible to bad influences; she ascertains if the society into which she wishes to conduct them be expedient and suitable for them, or at least, as everything in this world is relative, whether it may not be too advanced, too old for them. There are wines which may be drunk at forty which at eighteen will fly to the head. I dwell on this point, because there is not always sufficient consideration paid to this difference of age, of character, and of impressionability, which are constantly altering what is relatively good into what is relatively evil. Parents, in order to give a little knowledge of the world — and of a too precocious world — to their children, often destroy in them what is precious beyond measure, innocence and love of simplicity; they develop all the seeds of evil in their minds, and principally that inordinate love of pleasing, which may become later on the cause of bitter sorrow to them. My children, I am most anxious to exaggerate nothing; I desire to condemn nothing absolutely but what is undeniably evil. I wish only to reprove excesses; all, in a word, which reason, enlightened by Faith, must herself condemn. I will explain more fully my idea by an example that all can understand. Nothing is more delightful nor, oftentimes, more beneficial, than after the fiery heat of a summer's day to go out and breathe the cool, refreshing air of a beautiful evening; and yet good sense will prohibit a feverish patient from leaving his room, especially at night. What would you say, then, to a man with a constitution weakened by fever, who asked to go out with you under the pretext that a walk ought not to be hurtful to him any more than to you? And yet you do not see that you yourselves are more imprudent than that sick man; for under the pretext of training the mind and manners of your children, for things with which they will always become soon enough acquainted, you intentionally expose to serious moral dangers those characters not yet sufficiently formed; you infect them with a feverish longing for things more or less unwholesome, which may, if more fully developed later, poison their whole life. Be cautious then, my dear children; be most cautious in choosing what you would impart to your household, and particularly to your children. "She hath considered." Learn to examine, to weigh, to exercise moderation in everything.

You must also avoid those intimate fireside conversations in which fathers and mothers suffer themselves at times to speak of subjects in over plain terms, under the pretext that children do not understand or pay attention to what is said. Ask those who have the charge of youth, and they will tell you that the understanding of children of four or five is wonderfully in advance of their years, particularly for the comprehension of evil; and our daily experiences furnishes us with many sad proofs of this truth. Relate more or less scandalous stories before young children, veil the recital with a metaphor, and lull yourself with the pleasing but sad illusion that your children have understood nothing of it. Later on you will be astonished at discovering all that has sprung up in their hearts. The first seed of the accursed plant was perhaps that very half-hinted conversation which you allowed yourself to carry on in their presence, in a house where you imprudently took them. Those words, that conversation, that hint, that smile, lit up the whole horizon for them; they brought to life the seeds of evil, which are to be found in the hearts of all the children of Adam, and thus unconsciously you yourself prepared a sad future for your children. Alas! why do Christian parents so often forget this maxim of the Latin poet — "One cannot have too much regard for the innocence of a child; if you persist in wounding modesty, despise not youth, but let the thought of childhood rise up before you to check bad words and actions."[1]

I must also warn you to be careful about newspapers, books, and novels. Leave nothing lying about in your house which contains poison; your children may take it up at any moment when your back is turned. Have no bad books in your library, or should you possess any such, as by your age, or some other special reason you may be authorized to keep, have them always under lock and key. I have known the children of a good religious family ruined by books incautiously left on the open shelves of a library. Children have a propensity to evil stronger in them than an instinct for good; they possess a fine scent for certain things, and when once their mind has been awakened, they persist in following on the trail to the end — God only knows through what a path of thorns and briars! You cannot take too many precautions; I do not mean you to be spies; I mean you to be earnest watchers; and if you accuse me of being absurdly scrupulous and over particular, I shall be forced to conclude you know nothing of a child's heart and disposition.

[1] Juvenal, *Sat.* xiv.

If you are constant in following the counsels I have given, none of the interests of your family will be neglected by you; you will provide all that is necessary for them, and your home will become for your children and yourself a fountain of all good. You know that when a deep channel is hollowed out for a spring, it pours itself forth in profusion; its waters ever flow on in never-failing abundance, till by degrees it broadens, deepens, and finally becomes a great river. So will your house be; and I fervently pray that these words of the Sacred Book may be said of each and all of your families, and of their temporal and spiritual interests — "A little fountain grew into a very great river, and abounded into many waters."[1]

---

[1] Esth. xi. 10.

NINTH DISCOURSE

Developing firmness with constancy — The Valiant Woman is neither obstinate nor fickle.

She hath girded her loins with strength, and hath strengthened her arm. (Prov. 31:17)

MY CHILDREN,

The valiant woman exercises her activity not only in the interior of her house, where she is the glory and joy of her husband, where she presides with praiseworthy zeal over all the labors of the domestics, but she also keeps her eyes open to every source of material prosperity for her family; in concert with her husband she examines and deliberates over the properties, the vineyards, the fields which are for sale, and purchases them in accordance with the opportunities of the moment, the circumstances and resources of her family, and the prospects, which the objects that have excited in her a legitimate desire of acquisition may present. "She hath considered a field, and hath bought it: with the fruit of her hands she hath planted a vineyard." These last words point out with what care and persevering attention the mother of a family must devote herself to all the interests of her household, to the prudent amelioration of her property, to the reasonable and moderate augmentation of her income, and provision for her children's future; but religion imposes upon her the obligation of doing nothing contrary to honor and probity, nor of seeking to found her fortune on the success of skillfully disguised frauds, which can only merit one name in the language of justice and honesty.

The words of Scripture seem to attach a special importance to country life and all outdoor field work. Therefore, have I recommended to you, as a healthful and practically wise measure, country walks, and the contemplation of those varied and admirable scenes of nature where we find peace, order, wisdom, and tranquil happiness; and on this occasion I cannot pass over silently the culture of flowers — those excellent pencillings of the thoughts of the Divinity, those perfumed guests who speak to us so sweetly of virtue and our duties and who, even in the moment when they fall fading from their stalks, leave us a tender, yet melancholy, lesson on the fragility of human life. After having thus explained this text of Scripture, we raised our thoughts on high, and said that a woman was bound to make a provision for her family, not alone of bread and wine, but of all good things she might meet upon her way; and that she should amass with prudent carefulness treasures of spiritual benefits to pour them into her children's minds.

The verse which follows will require two discourses. "She hath girded her loins with strength, and hath strengthened her arm." What is strength? It may be defined as an energy of soul which enables us to bear calmly the trials and evils of life; which gives us courage to carry out our designs with unshaken firmness, and preserves in us a vigor of action which human obstacles cannot destroy. Saint Cyril styles it "an untiring energy which enables the mind to act with all the vigor of youth."[1] These different definitions are merely a commentary on the words of Scripture — "She hath girded her loins with strength, and hath strengthened her arm."

Firmness and strength of character are virtues which keep the middle path between the two opposite defects of obstinacy

[1] Cyril Alex. *in Isai.* l. v. t. iii. p. 1143, edit. Migné.

and weakness; and this is another proof of that important truth to which I have more than once called your attention. Virtue and vice are distinguished by the quantity of the dose: put the right quantity and you have a virtue; take away that quantity or exceed it and you have a vice. Listen to Saint Thomas, with his usual clearness and conciseness — "Obstinacy consists in keeping to one's own ideas and plans more than one ought; weakness, in not keeping to them enough; and firmness, in keeping to them as one ought."[1]

Have you never met with people so infatuated with themselves that everything they say or do must be right? Everything they dream of must be done, otherwise the world will go to ruin. Once an idea has entered their brain, it takes such hold that there is no room for a contrary opinion. This idea has very often its ridiculous side; no matter, it has got an entrance into that brain, taken up all the disposable space, and the omnibus is full. Respectable and elegant travellers — that is to say, just, true, and beautiful thoughts — present themselves in vain; the places are all occupied, and none can now enter. "If such minds," says Albert the Great, "should take it into their heads to maintain that it is night while the sun is shining, do not try to prove the contrary to them; you will only lose your time." Obstinacy, as moralists remark, is a proof of a weak mind, or at all events, it indicates an excessive self-love and wounded vanity. It is sufficient for some people that they have once publicly enunciated an opinion for them never after to retract it; even though it has been said without quite meaning it, in a moment of unreflecting passion, no matter, that is only an additional reason for their adding to it, and yet though they are quite sensible of the unreasonableness of their persistence in it. It is a sad truth to acknowledge, but it is not the less a truth, that it is not good sense and truth which oftenest govern men's understanding, but their passions, and above all, their embittered passions; and this is so certain, that you may actually make men pass successively from one opinion to the

[1] Summa 2a. 2æ. q. 128, a. 2.

contradictory one by attacking them on their weak point; and for this very reason, there is no more changeable character than an obstinate one. They are never so near altering their opinions as when most full of protestations of unswerving attachment to them. Wait a little while, and the new Proteus, so rigid and inflexible last night, will have already taken another form; the only thing that is essential is to let him have the satisfaction of believing that he alone, without any foreign influence, has wrought the metamorphosis. We need not be astonished at these changes; truth alone is fixed and stable, and obstinacy has no part in truth — it keeps not within its prudent bounds.

There are other natures placed at the opposite extreme; such as weak characters wanting in consistency. Like a sponge, they take in succession the color of the different liquids into which you plunge them. Put a sponge into a liquor of a deep black tinge and it will become black; then throw it into red, from that to white, and it will take the most dissimilar tints one after another. It is an emblem of certain dispositions, which through weakness, inability to resist, and sometimes of set purpose, will embrace an idea you propose to them, and say yes and no to the same question, like the wind which veers from north to south. It would be a curious study to follow such people into the different salons where shades of thought of the most opposite dyes prevail, and hear them exclaim in one, I am a mouse, look at my feet; in another, I am a bird, look at my wings. It would also be curious to note how, in the same conversation, they will speak for and against, according to this influence or that fear; how, through a desire of tacking, or simply through weakness, this fault of multiform yet undefined shapes makes a man yield the instant he meets with opposition or resistance. In weakness there is always much indolence, which contents itself with anything, provided it is allowed to slumber in peace.

Between obstinacy and weakness, the virtue of firmness takes the middle course, keeping to its ideas, projects, and resolutions, but only as much as should be done. When a firm character has once well examined and weighed its purpose before God; when it has consulted those whom providence has given it for its natural counselors; when it has taken all the precautions which Christian prudence suggests, then it goes straight to its end, and suffers nothing to stop it: neither the observations of men, nor the injustice of public opinion, nor the voice of the passions. Like the war-horse of Job — "He smelleth the battle afar off," and he saith, let us go! Firmness does not however exclude suppleness and docility of mind, and a readiness to admit new ideas which may perfect the old; for such is human weakness, and such the ignorance of our nature, that the finest minds cannot afford to remain fixed and immovable in one opinion to the point of refusing to entertain others which might circumscribe, limit, extend, or modify those they had already conceived. "True firmness," says Fénelon, "is gentle, humble, and tranquil. An angry, imperious, disquieted firmness is not worthy of being employed in the work of God."[1] When firmness possesses these conditions; when it is calm, peaceful, and guided by the Spirit of God, it is never excessive, it never pushes men or things to extremes; it knows how to compassionate and sympathize; it is like a finely tempered steel spring; it has all the strength and elasticity of skillfully prepared metal. It is strong, because founded on the true and the divine; it is ductile, because it is penetrated with humility; it is intelligent, because it is diffident of itself, and knows how to reverse its decisions when they have not been wisely matured.

I hear you raising a grave objection, and saying — "You are not removing the difficulty: Obstinacy is a defect which makes us hold to our own ideas and projects more than we ought; weakness gives them up without good reasons; firmness, on the contrary, is a quality which makes us maintain our own opinions as far as we ought to do; but where are we to find this precise point which Saint Thomas calls, 'as we

[1] *Lettres Spirit.* cx. t. viii. p. 533, edit. Leroux-Jouby.

ought to do?'" I acknowledge, my children, I should greatly rejoice could I discover for you some instrument wherewith you could measure these things exactly, and which would serve as an indication how best to blend a firm adhesion to the truth with a prudent diffidence of one's self; a disposition to stop, advance, or draw back, according to the opportuneness of events and the rules of true wisdom. There are such instruments for accurately mixing so many spoonfuls of oil, so many of vinegar, so many grains of salt. Unfortunately, in the moral order there exist no such instruments so precise and mathematically accurate; and therein lies the best answer to those narrow minds who would have everything conducted with absolute precision, and decisions laid down on the most rigid lines. As we advance in life, we become more and more suspicious of such a way of conducting or of cutting short all questions.

Let me briefly point out the precautions which prudence suggests. Have you reflected seriously before adopting such an idea, or following such a course? Have you consulted the persons in whom you ought to place confidence? Have you not that inflexibility which even in the path of good is a defect? Does not firmness degenerate in you into a kind of faith in your personal infallibility, which would spoil the best cause? Can you reconsider your opinion when you hear the warnings of wisdom and the testimony of competent persons? Another very essential question — are you calm when you are weighing a point? How does your pulse beat? Are you not somewhat excited? Agitation is undoubtedly not always a proof that we are in the wrong, but it shows we need time for reflection; it should induce us to wait awhile, to sleep a night, nay, many nights, on our project. Above all, examine well whether your pretended firmness does not arise from wounded self-love, rancor, or bitterness; and this may be easily recognized by a certain tone of abruptness, by restlessness, and an effervescence of temper, which seems to seek occasions of breaking forth, like pent up lava. "The strength which one draws from rancor and irritation," says Madame Swetchine, "is never aught but weakness."[1] Is not this your case? Do you not feel in all your faculties that irritable rigidity, that bronze-like tenacity, which cannot yield, and which refuses all flexibility of movement? If it be so, suspect your firmness a little; "for," says Fénelon, "true firmness is gentle, humble, and tranquil. The firmness which is marked by roughness, haughtiness, and disquietude is not worthy of being employed in the work of God. . . . Humble yourself," says again the great Archbishop, "but let it be without weakness."

Can it be said that, after having taken all these precautions, you will not sometimes commit an error in their application? Alas! my children, error is the lot of human nature; God alone is impeccable. You will undoubtedly still make mistakes; you will err, sometimes on the side of weakness, sometimes on that of obstinacy; but your errors at least will not be very dangerous, because you will have the power of recognizing them. God, who so loves us, will give you, when necessary, sufficient light to discover them; a wise diffidence of yourself will facilitate the entrance of divine wisdom into your souls, and you will have firmness enough to retrace your steps, and walk in the direction pointed out by the grace of God.

But if we can still err while taking all these precautions, what shall we say of those obstinate beings who follow their own notions only, who believe only in themselves, who are so completely wedded to one idea under the pretext of being true, that they end by falling into the most deplorable exaggerations? They do not reflect that it is possible to err even when carrying out a just and right persuasion, because in the intellectual world many ideas intersect, complete, and perfect each other, so that exclusiveness is a very bad system, and may lead to an abyss, even though one's hobby be in itself a good one. What are we to say of those little minds, those small vessels, so imbued with the one liquor they hold, that they cannot conceive the existence of a more generous or finer wine

1 *Lettres*, t. ii. p. 122.

than the one they contain? And therefore nothing finds entrance into them, because they are so full of themselves and of belief in their own merit. What are we to think of those abrupt characters, all acute angles, who mistake obstinacy for firmness, who dignify their ridiculous self-opinionatedness with the title of respect for one's self and one's dignity, and who would think themselves disgraced by an acknowledgment of having been in the wrong? Dispositions of such a sort resemble untamed horses, which, harnessed for the first time to a carriage, rush violently on, heeding neither rein nor guiding voice, and reach the foot of a mountain after having dashed everything to pieces, and perhaps endangered the lives of those who were so imprudent as to confide themselves to their care. Natures so constituted bring misfortune on their families and on society. They crush and destroy everything both in men and affairs, and there are some things which once crushed never recover. They alienate hearts and minds; and very often that state of suffering which weighs so heavy on families and social relations has no other source than that stupid obstinacy which knows not how to yield.

But how much sweeter, how much more Christian would life be, on the contrary, if all characters resembled the springs of well made carriages, which are strong enough to bear the heaviest burdens, yet yield so flexibly that one does not perceive the roughness of the road, but reposes as tranquilly as on a couch of down. Such are the characters formed in the school of the Gospel. They are strong to bear up against and resist every shock, and in order the better to withstand them, they often yield; yield with mingled force and gentleness: with force, because they are proof against the most violent shocks, and have hardly yielded when they spring back on themselves and resume their place; yet all this is done with so much softness and smoothness, that the traveller can sleep in peace. May you, my children, resemble in your homes those strong yet flexible springs! May all your family, husband, children, and servants, find repose in you! Your part in this world is to be the springs of your household; be therefore strong, perfectly smooth, and, above all, well oiled. The coach will then roll tranquilly on, with occasional jolts it is true, for such are inevitable in this world; but those very jolts will only show how perfect are the springs. At the moment of the shock you will bend noiselessly, yield without an effort, and the shock once passed, resume quietly your ordinary place. Your husband, though he may be of a difficult temper, will end by admiring what he did not always comprehend, and in some moment or other of expansion and candor he will say, in speaking of you — "What an excellent spring my house possesses! How flexible! How gracefully elastic! and at the same time how well tempered is its strength, which can yield to me while resisting, and resist me while yielding! I should be truly unreasonable were I to complain!" If, on the contrary, you persist in being a rigid and immovable spring, the shock, which must infallibly come, will surely break the iron, scatter the coach, and, unless the accident remain a secret, which rarely comes to pass, you will furnish conversation, and probably amusement, for the public at your expense.

Before concluding this first discourse on firmness, I must say one word on a defect which is most opposed to it, which troubles our whole lives, and makes of our existence one perpetual, ever-flowing tide, agitated by violent winds; I mean susceptibility. This is a subject which is perhaps not sufficiently treated in books, and on which I particularly desire to dwell for a few moments; for this defect or infirmity, whichever it may be, is often the sole cause of the unhappiness of life. What, then, is susceptibility? It is difficult to define an airy sylph, to calculate the direction of the winds at sea, the caprices of the imagination, or the dreams of a man in fever, but it is still more difficult to define susceptibility, or to account for its various metamorphoses. Susceptibility is derived from a Latin word signifying a faculty of receiving impressions. Have you ever remarked persons suffering from rheumatism? They dread the slightest currents of air, — and unfortunately for them everything is a current of air — the least breeze, the slightest noise, all jars on their nerves and makes them ill. Susceptibility is a species of rheumatism in our moral nature: everything fatigues these poor invalids; everything wounds them; everything becomes a current of air to give them fever. Go to the right, and they are hurt; to the left, and they are dreadfully offended.[1] The slightest act, the most inoffensive words, assume gigantic proportions in their eyes. If you are chatting merrily, it must be of them you are speaking; if you keep silence, you are gloomy and out of sorts about something they have done; if you smile, you must be laughing at them; if you are grave, you have some pique against them; if through natural absence of mind, or some preoccupation, you appear to maintain a reserved silence towards them, though in quite an unimportant matter, or perhaps unintentionally, these invalids maintain that you have entirely forgotten them, and set aside the most sacred duties of affection. It is in vain that the truest and most sincere devotion lies in your inmost heart for them, of which they have many times had proof; nothing can cure that weary brain of its rash suspicions. What can I tell you to do? It is as impossible to satisfy such people as to know for certain the course of the equinoctial gales: with the best will in the world, you have only to resign yourselves to bear the outbursts of their ill-humor and discontent.

Susceptibility indicates great weakness of mind and character, or else a very large amount of self-love, and occasionally both these defects united. Strong minds are not susceptible; they are of too vigorous a mold to let themselves be affected by those manifold petty trifles, those countless grains of sand, which form, as it were, the sum of human life. A susceptible mind is always unhappy; it is as impressionable as a sensitive plant, and agitated by every passing breath of wind; and even with every possible precaution, life on this

---

[1] "Life with a susceptible person is like a journey by moonlight with a shy horse, which takes fright at every bush." — Father Faber's *Conferences*, p. 273.

Ninth Discourse

earth is so constituted, that there must always exist slight currents of air in the atmosphere of souls, and often violent shocks to overwhelm those vacillating characters, which have no more consistency than the leaves of the forest. I might address the words of Saint Chrysostom to those who are so easily affected by every little thing, and say: "It is not the nature of things, it is the weakness of your own minds which occasions your pain."[1] No, it is not the nature of things, it is not that person who is the cause of your grief; she never even thought about you; but an unfortunate notion got into your head, and cannot be got out again; therein is the sole cause of your unhappiness. No, it is not your friend who is so truly attached to you, whom you ought to accuse, it is the buzzing of your own brain, it is the power of your own imagination to create these phantoms. I grant you that these phantoms actually do exist, but the grand manufactory for their production is to be found in your own head; it is there you must apply the remedy. And even if there should really be some flies floating around you in the air, are we to pay attention to flies in this world? Do we fight with every insect that buzzes about us? That would give us too much to do, besides being trouble lost. A pagan philosopher has given us the sagest counsels on this subject "The noblest manner of forgiving," says Seneca, "is to ignore the wrong done." "Credulity does much harm; and very often it is best not even to listen to it, for in some things it is better to be deceived than to be suspicious. You must banish from your mind every conjecture, every suspicion, every source of unjust anger. Such a person saluted me coldly, such another behaved impolitely to me; this one rudely interrupted the sentence I had begun, that other did not invite me to his entertainment, while the countenance of some one else seemed ungracious towards me. Pretexts for suspicion are never wanting: let us look more simply at things, and judge them more kindly."[2] The same

---

[1] *In Epist. ad Cor. Hom. xlii.* n. v. t. x. p. 620.
[2] *De Irâ*, l. ii. chs. xxiii. xxiv.

philosopher tells us of a Sybarite of his time who complained of a bruise he had received from sleeping on crumbled rose-leaves.[1] There are many people in this world to whom nothing that could insure happiness seems wanting, but their own susceptibility is an obstacle interposing itself at every moment between them and external objects; they resemble not a little Seneca's fastidious gentleman; everything wearies them, even rose-leaves, if they have often slept on them.

Whilst walking before my cottage by the sea-shore, I have sometimes remarked a fact from which I have drawn the following moral deduction — The blackbirds and other timid songsters on seeing me advance, though with the most pacific intentions, and without even thinking of them, give vent to a loud cry of terror, and fly off wildly into the bushes; one would really say they suspected me of the most hostile intentions. But the cause of their fright is in their own imagination, and their safest plan would be to make no noise, but remain quiet on their branch while I pass; then I should not be even aware of their presence, and they would be most effectually protected by silent repose. Is not this a faithful portrait of susceptible characters? You are walking tranquilly in the paths of life, when suddenly, without any apparent reason, they scream out loudly; one would think you had declared war to the knife against them, which you most certainly have not the slightest idea of doing. All the commotion is in their own imagination. Susceptibility, my children, may spring from the nerves, the constitution, a diseased imagination. What a number of sensitive people are to be found in this world! The best counsel I can give them is, to cast aside half, and even sometimes three quarters, of their own impressions, or still better, reject them altogether; then only will they arrive at the truth. I would also wish them to possess a sincerely devoted friend, in whom they could have perfect confidence, and to whom they could confide all their wounded feelings; but on this one condition, of permitting the most entire frankness to their friend, and showing him a child-like submission.

[1] *Ibid.* ch. xxv.

Ninth Discourse

Susceptibility, as we have already said, springs also very often from self-love; and even where other causes exist, self-love and wounded vanity are ordinarily the chief components in the mixture.

There are some natures so imbued with vanity that they imagine all the world must be thinking of them. This is an instinct of self-love, an unhappy idea which everywhere pursues them; if they are overlooked for a single instant, all the obligations of politeness are thrown aside. Woe to you if you are so imprudent as to neglect offering up some grains of incense at their shrine, or perhaps even the censer full! Woe to you if a word of criticism, though kindly meant, escape you; or if at some *soirée* you omit, by some involuntary forgetfulness, to present them with that bouquet of falsehoods, which is styled compliments, you are sure to draw on yourself a flood of rancor and bitterness, or at least to have stored up against you a provision of suppressed anger which will not fail to explode on an early opportunity.

Humility, my children, is not only a great virtue, it is also a source of good sense, peace, and happiness. The humble-minded must be happy. What profound peace we enjoy when we can do without creatures, their lying words, and their deceitful praises! How happy we are when we can, if needful, place ourselves under the feet of others to be trampled at will, without feeling hurt! Nature cannot understand this language; nevertheless, it is the language of faith, and reason, and of true happiness. Whether we like it or not, we must often resign ourselves to being trodden under foot in this world. Whether we like it or not, evil tongues, treachery, calumny, and injurious proceedings will make of us a carpet on which others will tread with malicious pleasure. We may undergo this fate without anger or serious annoyance; it is perfectly reconcilable with the dignity of a Christian and the nobility of resignation; and there is even true grandeur in lifting ourselves up again, and saying with that emperor — "I do not even feel myself hurt." Indifference to a number of earthly things is the secret of a Christian's science and the principal cause of the serenity of a just soul.

One word more of counsel, and I have done. If you live with susceptible characters, treat them with gentle kindness blended with firmness. Be compassionate, but fear not to make them sometimes touch with their own hands the windmills they mistake for armed warriors coming to attack them. If a horse be shy, you lead him up to the very spot of his imagined peril, and cure him by letting him see how chimerical his fears are. But as there are things which cannot be wholly cured in this world, you must cultivate patience and forbearance, and avoid as much as possible what may cause them agitation. There are people whose heads are bad, whose brains are somewhat weak; and Saint Augustine remarked long ago — "The weaker a mind, the more easily it is offended."[1] Charity wills that we have pity on such people, and not knowingly expose them to difficulties, which, although in reality only grains of sand, take in their imagination the form of lofty mountains. I do not say you will altogether avoid paining them; that would be a standing miracle, and I only ask what is possible and feasible. Therefore, if you live with such characters, be provided with a waterproof mantle, for you will need it in moments of unexpected torrents.

I trust, my children, that these first observations may have somewhat enlightened you and prepared you to comprehend the virtue of strength, for it is one of the most valuable qualities women can possess. Much more remains to be developed; I reserve it for our next meeting, when, it may be, you will come to understand what a sublime doctrine and practical teaching is contained in the praise the Scripture bestows on the valiant woman — "She hath girded her loins with strength, and hath strengthened her arm."

---

1 *De Doctr. Christ.* l. ii. n. 20, p. 53.

TENTH DISCOURSE
The Valiant Woman has the strength from God to overcome whatever evil with goodness and gentleness of heart.

She hath girded her loins with strength, and hath strengthened her arm. (Prov. 31:17)

MY CHILDREN,

Strength, or fortitude, as I before told you, is that energy of mind which makes us bear the burdens and ills of this life calmly, which gives us courage to carry out our designs with unshaken firmness, and maintains us in that vigor of action which human obstacles cannot arrest. Again, every quality has two defects resembling it, which stand on either side at right and left; the one errs through excess, the other through deficiency. This maxim is peculiarly applicable to strength and firmness of character, for obstinacy overleaps the bounds of true strength, because it holds to its own ideas beyond what is true and right, thereby degenerating into weakness — a weakness as replete with danger as is the engine which runs off the rails. Weakness, properly so called, is, on the contrary, the failing of inconsistent people, who take any form we wish, and become tinged with every shade of opinion in succession. This last defect is sometimes the result of shrewd calculation on the part of those chameleon-like natures, who change their colors according to the position and reflections of the sun. They possess in their wardrobes half a dozen different opinions, which they put on by turns, as the actor does his costumes. Betwixt obstinacy and weakness stands true firmness, "keeping to our own ideas and projects, as we ought," says Saint Thomas — an expression full of sense and largeness, fixing nothing in an absolute manner, but abandoning the solution to circumstances which will themselves be regulated by practical good sense.

I also pointed out to you, before concluding these explanations, another defect which is opposed to strength of character, and even paralyzes its action. I mean susceptibility. In fever the skin becomes so tender that we are obliged to guard the sick person from the least breath of air; and in susceptible natures we may say that the skin of the soul is acted on by a moral fever, whose attacks are redoubled by the faintest breeze. It would be almost necessary to wrap up such beings in cotton wool, and even then I believe they would, by their untiring restlessness, end by irritating the skin with the very down.

Let us continue this important subject today, my children, and finish our commentary on the verse, "She hath girded her loins with strength, and hath strengthened her arm."

The sea-fish has its shell, the soldier his buckler, and the ship its girdle of iron. The mind should also possess its buckler and its girdle — its buckler is strength, and its girdle is firmness. Strength is a necessity, for it is daily required, not always for action, but more especially to bear up against and withstand shocks from without and misfortunes from within. The bridge of stone suspended across a vast river does not act: It is motionless but yet strong, because it can bear much; it can resist the rapid current, the effect of the atmosphere, the weight of vehicles and passengers, and also its own weight. All these united burdens form one enormous load, of which engineers alone can compute the extent. See, likewise, that beam: it alone, had it feeling, could know the weight it sustains; it alone could complain of it, because it alone is aware of its own work of resistance. So, too, in man the principal exercise of strength consists in supporting the events of life and in bearing with himself. This first and chief employment for strength of character is what demands the most energy and perseverance; it is latent, and no one discovers it, no one suspects its existence. But the heart of man is often like a beam about to give way at the very moment when the world deems him happy and exempt from sorrows, precisely because everything connected with the exercise of this internal force is mysteriously hidden and invisible. What a daily expenditure of courage some souls have thus made! How many hearts continually sweat tears of blood in their interior lives, of which no trace appears externally! Happily that which most attracts the eye of Heaven, which is most cherished by the angels, which our Saviour holds most in account, is that same interior life which blossoms in secret, hidden from the eyes of men, and which has never been sullied by the influence of the world's corrupting vanity — it is this which falls drop by drop from our hearts and passes directly into the heart of God. "Thy Father, who seeth in secret, hears you."[1] Yes; there is a Father on high whose heart is overflowing with love, who sees all and knows all; and when once a soul has taken firm hold of this thought, she is strong, because she can say with a holy anchorite — "I can, if necessary, be alone with God in this world; for no man ever said in his heart, 'I am alone with God in the world,' and had not peace."[2] When strength has to be visibly exercised, when it has to strike and act as a warrior, or struggle against obstacles like an iron-clad vessel, it requires much less moral force; for human nature is so constituted that action of itself excites courage, and the stirring movement of the first bound has the property of developing increased vigor. Perhaps there are also innumerable considerations of self-love which have something to say to the energy of action.

Physical strength, in different degrees, is necessary for every movement of the body, and is required every hour in the

---

[1] Matt. 6:4.
[2] *Apopht. Patr. Patrol. Græc* t. lxv. p. 134.

day. Moral strength is, in the same way, daily and hourly needed. Man requires it to fight against the difficulties of life, the dangers of the world, the reverses of fortune, family jars, interior tribulations, and those countless forms of suffering, anxiety, and anguish, which besiege man from his cradle upwards, and form in phalanx around him, like those winged insects we find in marshy places.

But putting aside this general point of view, to which I only meant to allude, I wish to dwell more particularly on the uses of strength in women's lives.

We have distinguished between two kinds of strength — strength to act and strength to bear; it is the latter, especially, of which you have most need. I spoke just now of a bridge which crowds of people are constantly crossing, and which has to support the effect of the atmosphere, the fury of the waves, the weight of all that rests on it, without counting that of the stone of which it is constructed. Is not this an image of woman's life? Is not the wife a sort of bridge for the family? Does not everyone lean a little on her — husband, children, servants, even troublesome neighbors; while a large portion of domestic cares rolls also over her, and weighs continually on her shoulders. When the honeymoon is past, my children, you may find yourself with a husband whose habits, character, and tastes will be antagonistic to yours; who, even when least intending it, will jar on your nerves, whose every word will irritate you, whose very presence will excite in you an ill feeling, and in whom it is probable you excite feelings of a similar nature, and so (for such impressions are ordinarily reciprocal) an antipathetic fluid passes from your heart to his, and from his to yours. I am far from supposing that this state of feeling is so enduring as to be prejudicial to that family affection which is essential; but it occurs often enough to weary, or at least deeply sadden the heart. You will, then, need strength not only to keep you from yielding to that feverish irritation, and to help you to bear, but also to grind to atoms your self-love. Your antipathies must be bruised like the olive, in order to be changed into the oil of kindly acts, which are the unctuous produce of your charity. This employment of strength, until it is finally changed into oil, is the surest means of lessening the rudeness of shocks, and of softening your husband's heart as soon as it begins to harden, or even of reviving an affection which had begun to cool. Your children will try your patience: For you may have to deal with characters which, though excellent at bottom, are difficult in temper and peevish in humor; with good hearts but not overmuch brains, the very variety of whose whims will be a torment to you. Take every morning and evening five grains of that strength which endures with patience; be calm yet firm, gentle yet vigilant — then you may act with all the tranquillity of conscious power. Your servants will complete the picture. You will have to complain of their stubbornness, ill temper, too independent spirit; what am I saying? perhaps even of their incapacity, want of virtue, and unbearable dispositions. I am far from wishing that you should retain them if their deficiencies reach a point which it is impossible to pass over. I do not forbid remonstrances, kindly reproofs, and, when necessary, correction more or less severe; but, before all, I insist on patient strength and forbearing firmness, which knows how to wait; for this is oftentimes the best and most energetic means of attaining your end.

It will not only be your husband, children, and servants who will try you, but also your friends and acquaintances. You counted on such a person. She proved a reed to pierce your hand — not, perhaps, the first, but the second time you leant upon her. Where, then, are friends in this world? It is asserted that a woman rarely — I do not like to say never — finds a true and steady friend in the heart of another woman. Moral philosophers explain this difficulty by numerous considerations of natural antipathies and secret causes of vanity; for it is rare to find two lights shining with equal brilliancy at the same moment; and, because of that indefinable something fragile existing in flowers and all constructions of glass. "There is an immense amount of friendship necessary between two women," says Madame Swetchine, "to prevent the weakness of jealousy in her who is the inferior."[1] We admit that you may meet with steady female friends, but we must add, to speak truly, that they are rare. You reckoned on that heart as on your own; well, one day a vague rumor reaches you, then arises a suspicion, finally certainty. That person has betrayed you again and again more or less seriously; she has been faithless to all that is most sacred in friendship. This startling intelligence comes like a great wave against the ship of your soul, and what a blow it strikes on the heart! At other times your relatives are the cause: what miseries, what secret antipathies! Each one suffers in his turn, and very often those who cry out the loudest are not themselves the least full of thorns. Later on you will meet enemies, for who has not enemies in this world? You have made an enemy of such a person by doing them a service; for with some natures there is no greater crime than that of putting them under an obligation, and condemning them to that position of inferiority in which gratitude places them. Such a one is jealous of you for no other reason but because you possess some quality or other, or because you are too attractive to please her. "Why do you attack me?" said the glow-worm to an insect as ugly as it was venomous. "Because you shine so brightly," replied the other. This answer is the true explanation of a vast amount of hatred, irritation, and revenge. There is so much bitterness in the human heart by the side of such noble instincts! So much mean jealousy beside so much love for all that is noble and good! Perhaps you yourself, too, often make a vain display of your qualities, exaggerating them, or, at all events, boring the public by having the air of laying yourself out for their admiration, for there is nothing of which men tire so quickly as of the exhibition of their neighbor's good qualities. We are easily forgiven a display of faults and follies, because such a view places the spectator in a position of superiority over us; but what is with difficulty

---

[1] *Lettres*, t. i. p. 66.

Tenth Discourse

forgiven is the possession of sterling good qualities, if they at all throw the pretensions of others into the shade. I might continue this description, going with you through the various events of life, and showing you everywhere the waves which threaten to demolish your vessel, to break up its fastenings, and finally submerge it. Your ship has, therefore, need of being perfectly well built; its compartments of stout timber must be solidly put together, and, should you venture into certain seas, have it plated with iron.

We have not yet arrived at your most formidable enemy, which enemy is yourself. Yes; to bear with one's self at certain times, to resist the disorder of one's own imagination, the shock to one's heart, to support the inertia and torpor of one's character, to sustain the soul during those days when she asks herself why she exists — during those weeks in which she feels more acutely the prison of her body, the hardness of her exile, the weight of her chain; when a thousand chimerical dreams torture her, when it seems as though a keen sword of anguish was separating our flesh and blood, our soul and mind — then is the hour of real combat, the moment when the most determined courage is required.[1] One can bear with one's husband, one's children, one's servants, even one's enemies; but this unhappy self, often so strange, so whimsical, so inconstant — this is the heaviest burden of all, and all the more heavy because it never quits us for one single instant. We may escape from husband, children, friends, and relatives, but this miserable self is an iron weight affixed by nature to our feet on the day of our birth, the chain of which no mortal hand is strong enough to loose.

I now come to a delicate subject, from which I have already lifted the veil, and whose leading features I partly sketched at our first meeting. "Ah, me! how weak a thing the

---

[1] "The narration of my interior revolutions, changes of government, civil wars, anarchy, despotism, and gleams of liberty would be a long one. These are annals which write themselves in deeply graven letters in the soul and furrows on the brow. Sometimes I, too, become worn out like an old dynasty." — *Lettres de Maurice de Guérin*, p. 323, fourth edition.

heart of woman is!" says the English tragedian.[1] Be good enough to hear me to the end before condemning what I have to say to you. Flesh and bones are necessary to the human body, and flesh naturally is and must be softer than the bones. In the same way in the plans of the Creator, in the magnificent ideal of the union of man and woman, two different characters were necessary — one strong, the other weak; and though sin deranged this primitive order, it could not destroy its foundations. Woman's mission requires something more gentle in mind and manner, something more elastic, more resembling a tendril which bends and twines, and thus more easily becomes an ornament to the tree from which it hangs. If this world consisted solely of rock, there would be no beauty, no variety, only an intolerable monotony. And this gentleness of heart when kept within the limits of virtue and wisdom, is the most attractive portrait of the goodness of God. The family would be incomplete, even from a moral point of view, without women; for there are influences which ought to be, and yet which could not be exerted, if the house contained only the manly character of the husband.

You see, my children, that I am not a very stern accuser. But this more pliable and elastic nature of women may and often does degenerate, especially in this our present age, into weakness — a weakness more or less blamable and more or less deplorable in its results. Does this arise from the effeminate and too easy manner in which young girls are brought up — to the absence of true and solid religious principles? Or are we to accuse the feverish ideas, the unceasing tumult of men and things, which transform society into an ever-rolling wave? It is a fact that characters have become enervated, and that this weakness of mind and want of energy makes itself most felt among women. Again, are we to attribute this sad result to those enervating writings which more and more deteriorate minds, and to those chimerical dreams which are the most powerful dissolvents of moral strength? I believe that the

[1] Shakespeare, *Julius Cæsar*, act ii. scene 4.

Tenth Discourse

union of all these different causes contributes to produce this effect, and in these times more particularly we might, despite many praiseworthy exceptions, repeat the words of the poet — "Ah, me! how weak a thing the heart of woman is!" This weakness is the cause of another defect with which women are often reproached — obstinacy. "I have known hundreds of women," says Montaigne (and it is thought Gascon women have a special prerogative herein), "whom you could sooner have got to eat a piece of red-hot iron than to retract an opinion uttered in anger."[1] It is possible that Montaigne's observation applies equally well to all lands, and that women everywhere run a risk of falling into the pitfall of obstinacy. When an idea has once fixed itself in their heads, it leaves indelible traces, and too often, alas, no place for any other, no matter how good and perfect that other may be. They are wholly penetrated with their notion, and you could sooner break them in pieces than induce them to yield an inch. Beware, my children, of obstinacy. You will easily recognize it by this sign: When you feel your head growing hot, your disposition becoming unbending, your whole being rising in revolt against the slightest contradiction, say instantly to yourself: Let me beware, these are the symptoms of the fever of obstinacy; I feel its first advances. Then kneel at the foot of the Cross and say to God — O Lord, defend me against myself, against my own weakness and obstinacy; penetrate my soul with Your grace, that it may never harden, but ever preserve in me an intelligent and kindly docility. Woman is weak from nature, from constitution, and in consequence of the education she receives.[2] And yet, let the mind of a woman be ennobled by a generous devotion, above all, let the love of her Saviour be enkindled in her soul, and she becomes capable of all that is most elevated in thought, most noble in heart, most heroic in courage, and most persevering in combat. "There are some women," says Saint Chrysostom, "who have not only

---

[1] *Essais*, l. ii. ch. xxxii.
[2] Cyril Alex. *Hom. Pasch.* xxviii. t. x. p. 947.

shown themselves more courageous than men, but who have almost attained to the impassibility of angels. There are some who, like a steadfast rock, are not only undisturbed by the fury of the waves, but who even force the foaming waters to break harmlessly around them; theirs is the strength of iron and the transparent hardness of the diamond."[1] Yes, my children, if nature has not endowed you in the same degree as men with active, moral strength, a work of transfiguration may be wrought in you by grace which will communicate to you, more especially, the strength of patience, the strength of judicious quietude, and, in a word, the strength of the rock on the sea-shore, which sees the furious waves rushing on, rearing their towering crests against it, yet remains immovable, and soon beholds the roaring waters dispersed in foam around its base. It is this power of long-suffering which I most particularly recommend to you. You will rarely meet occasions of exercising active force; but should the occasion present itself, you will be enabled, like the valiant woman, "to strengthen your arm," and direct its movements in action prudently and energetically; but show your strength habitually by unruffled sweetness, by abnegation and self-sacrifice. Seek to imbibe at the foot of the Cross, in your Communions, and in your meditations, that tenacious clinging to what is right, which will make of you domestic heroines. Men will take no count of your sufferings, nor of the drops of blood running from your heart and falling on the pavement of your hidden life; but God counts them every one, and angels will gather them up. Each unseen tear thus falling from your heart is changed into a pearl of great price; and what a happiness for you to find hereafter an incalculable multitude of such pearls in heaven, forming themselves into a thousand rays of glory and bliss wherewith to adorn your brows! This crown will be all the more beautiful and glorious, the weaker has been the nature of her who has thus gloriously conquered.[2]

[1] *De stud. præsent*, Hom. v. n. 3. t. xii. pp. 495, 496.
[2] Saint Augustine *Sermon cclxxxi*. t. v. p. 1669.

Tenth Discourse

Where shall you find means, my children, to acquire this spirit of strength? I know none better than confidence in God, and recourse to Him in those circumstances wherein you feel your forces failing. Undoubtedly, we must not despise the resources of natural wisdom, nor the counsels of prudence, but the heart of God is the true source whence a Christian soul derives courage. "The Lord is my rock, and my strength, and my saviour."[1] Lean then on God, as one leans on the arm and on the heart of a friend, and true strength will never fail you. There may be faintness in the inferior portion of your being, weariness in the imagination, and disturbance in the senses, but the nobler part of the soul will always preserve its serenity, and that is the main thing in virtue; the rest is but an accessory, which not only does not destroy true merit, but even augments and renders it more pleasing to God. When you feel the waters of tribulation closing over your heart, or *ennui* about to attack you with the virulence of an inveterate enmity, go and seek help at the foot of the Cross. Say to God — Yes, I accept all: I will all that Thou willest; I resign myself to endure all, provided that I never cease to love and be united to Thee. You will always arise with a renewed courage and a power of action of which you had never dreamed. "The serenity of the just man," says Saint Gregory the Great, "is aptly compared to that of the lion, for when attacked, he, too, retires into an impregnable fortress, that of his own mind; and he knows that he must be victorious over his enemies, for he loves that only of which none can deprive him against his will."[2]

Be you also like the lion, my children; have the same tranquil security. The lion fears nothing, and is calmly confident. Such is the nature God has given him; and these same qualities of strength and confidence He also communicates to His faithful servants: ". . .The just, bold as a lion, shall be without dread."[3]

---

[1] 2 Kings 22:2.
[2] *Morals*, l. xxxi. cap. xxviii. t. ii. p. 605, edit Migné.
[3] Prov. 28:1

The Valiant Woman

Again, the valiant soul may be compared to an island with bare and desolate shores, but in the interior rich, fertile, and firmly set. Do you resemble this happy isle! And amidst the bitter waters which surround you (and each one must have his portion of them), amidst the waves which threaten the fragile bark of your life, draw back into the interior of the island, that is, into the secret depths of your own heart, make for yourself a hidden sanctuary, with door ever closed, and you will not even hear the voices of the tempest. You will sing in all security the canticle of the Prophet — "The Lord is my firmament, my refuge, and my deliverer;"[1] "God is my strong one, in Him will I trust;"[2] and "I shall not be moved."[3]

---

[1] Ps. 17:3.
[2] II Kings 22:3.
[3] Ps. 61:7.

Eleventh Discourse
Goodness enlarges the heart of the Valiant Woman. She has that tranquillity of order which is the essence of peace.

She hath tasted and seen that her traffic is good: her lamp shall not be put out in the night. She hath put out her hand to strong things: and her fingers have taken hold of the spindle. (Prov. 31:18, 19)

MY CHILDREN,

The virtue of strength of purpose finds itself placed between two contradictory defects, and must therefore always steer a middle course. On one hand is obstinacy, which clings to its own ideas beyond the limits of good sense and prudence; on the other, weakness or pusillanimity, which constantly varies its opinions according to external influences, or according to the calculations of self-love and human respect. Between these two defects stands that strength of character which keeps steadfast to its own ideas in a fitting degree. It first reflects, consults, and examines; but its decision once taken, goes straight to its end without troubling itself about the opinions of others. Nevertheless, it does not forget that man is not infallible, and must therefore endeavor to preserve a certain suppleness and docility of mind and heart, in order to be able to modify his ideas, to profit by good advice, and to retract any involuntary errors. After pointing out the proper means for preventing these errors, in so far at least as human infirmity allows, I alluded to a very common defect, and one quite opposed to the virtue of firmness — I mean susceptibility.

In a second discourse, devoted likewise to comments on the same verse, I showed by casting a rapid glance over human life, and over woman's life in particular, how necessary to her is this quality of firmness, how it is needed in everyday intercourse, and the more so, because weakness of character and want of moral courage are failings with which women are generally reproached; failings, however, which may be changed into heroic virtues, if, under the influence of divine grace, a woman will only bring into play all those powerful and tenacious springs and resources which form part of her nature. Finally, I spoke of confidence in God and abandonment of ourselves into the arms of His divine providence as the principal means whereby to rivet strength of purpose in our inmost being, and to make our lives an illustration of those words of Scripture — ". . . the just, bold as a lion, shall be without dread."[1]

Here is the continuation of the text — "She hath tasted and seen that her traffic is good: Her lamp shall not be put out in the night. She hath put out her hand to strong things, and her fingers have taken hold of the spindle."

"She hath tasted and seen that her traffic is good." Virtue has its trials and tribulations in this world, but it has also its joys and lawful pleasures; and as long as these joys remain subservient to virtue, and do not aspire to rule the soul to the prejudice of their lawful mistress — as long as everything is referred to God, and tends towards Him as towards our last, chief end, the joys of virtue, and the legitimate satisfaction which the retrospection of good works and the success of undertaken labors bring to the soul, are among the rewards granted to the just man, and the severest moralist cannot condemn them. "Joy is the necessary companion of virtue," says Saint Thomas, "and to be truly virtuous we must do good with rejoicing, . . . and for this reason, that were virtue melancholy,

[1] Prov. 28:1.

we could not endure it long."[1] The very sight of good enlarges the heart, gives courage to the weak, and adds a hundred-fold to our strength; the soul experiences somewhat of that ineffable satisfaction which thrilled the heart of the Almighty at the first view of the creation — "And God saw all the things that He had made, and they were very good."[2] Yes, I love to see the valiant woman, after days and weeks of toil and labor, rejoicing over the success which has attended her efforts, tasting the delights of duties fulfilled, contemplating with satisfaction the tranquillity of her home, the good order reigning in her household, the harmony and calm presiding over the peaceable development of every undertaking, the gradual expanding of each character under her charge. She not only contemplates this spectacle, but she enjoys it, she imbibes its full flavor, she is made happy by it. This is what is signified by the words — "She hath tasted and seen." "When our heart is made glad by what is good, a great gift of God is given us," says Saint Augustine.[3] And a great doctor infers from this that we must do with joy and cheerfulness whatever we have to do, for that is the true way of doing good and of doing it well.

Vanity and folly may undoubtedly abuse these maxims, and render intensely ridiculous what in itself is most wise and conformable to the rules of true piety. One meets with characters so vainglorious, that they are always mistaking the chimeras of their own brain for realities, and believe themselves in some most favorable position when they are on the point of shipwreck: Like the unhappy man on whom, without his own knowledge, a miserable illusion was practiced, until he was made to take for magnificent, real buildings, the houses of cards which he was given to admire as his future inheritance. Yes, man has the melancholy talent of deceiving himself, or of allowing others to impose on him the grossest errors with the greatest facility, provided only they be flatter-

---

[1] *Ethics*, l. i. lect. xiii.; l. viii. lect. vi.
[2] Gen. 1:31.
[3] *In Psalm cxviii. Serm. xvii.* n. 1, t. iv. p. 1883.

ing to his self-love. He whose affairs are in a very bad way indeed imagines that they are so prosperous as to excite general envy; the fickle man praises in himself the firmness which can withstand every trial; the hedgehog believes himself charming, and the hare boasts of his warlike valor. A list of this world's illusions would be too long for detail here; each one can see through the errors and imaginations of others, but does not always even suspect the existence of his own. However it may be with those incontestible miseries of our poor human nature, it is not the less true that it is allowable to rejoice in what is really good, and with Christian modesty to glorify ourselves in God for it. "Let him who glories, glory in the Lord."[1] If this be not so, then we must also say that because the eye of the body is subject to optical delusions, we must never let ourselves be arrested by delight and admiration before beautiful pictures or the lovely scenes of nature. No one assuredly will desire to admit such an inference; errors and abuses prove nothing against the lawful use of things.

I cannot conclude my explanation of these words of Holy Writ — "She hath tasted and seen that her traffic is good" — without giving you counsel very necessary for your peace and happiness. As a rule, do not glorify yourself even for what is undeniably good; you might have done so beneficially and with impunity in a terrestrial paradise, where the gifts of one creature were to another only a cause of joy and thanksgiving to the great Creator. But in our actual world, where jealousy, malignity, and perfidy are the leading qualities in many characters — qualities placed, too, at the guidance of a narrow, malevolent spirit — I recommend to you the utmost discretion and the strictest prudence. Hide as much as you can the well-being of your family, for there are minds to whom the sight of the prosperity and happiness of others is a reason for hatred and the foulest accusations. Hide your success, or at least cause it to be forgiven you by your rare modesty; in so far as depends on you, be like the

[1] 2 Cor. 10:17.

Eleventh Discourse

little streamlet which conceals itself beneath the drooping ferns. Distrust those proud and jealous natures to whom the prosperity of another ever seems a direct personal attack on themselves and their own thirst for distinction. Live in and for your own family; unfold your thoughts and opinions to a small circle of true friends, and use caution in the choice of them. It is far from my idea to advise a misanthropic bearing or an exaggerated reserve, which would only be an obstacle to the practice of works of charity; what I recommend is merely that even balancing of all things; that prudent temperament which, while ever doing good, yet takes precautions against the malice of men and the poisoned fangs of jealousy and envy, which we meet at every turning in life.

The Wise Man adds — "The lamp of the valiant woman shall not be put out in the night." Following the literal sense, we should naturally be again led to speak of the activity of the woman who sleeps little, rises early, and is thus the first of her household to awake. But the subject is too delicate a one to revert to, and besides I hope I have already said enough to make converts of all women of good-will, and who have not yet sealed a compact with their morning pillow for the rest of their days. Let us, then, take these words of Scripture in another meaning, what the Doctors of the Church call an anagogical sense, that is, ascending from beneath to above — leaving a material element to attain a more elevated conclusion.

Happy the woman whose lamp is not put out in the night! Happy the woman who still preserves some noble ideas amid the invasion of material things; whose heart remains elevated above the flat, monotonous plains of life! Happy the woman whose Christian faith is a lamp which keeps on ever shining through the night of this world, through the darkness of passion and unbelief! "Her lamp shall not be put out in the night." Yes, my children, guard the lamp of your hearts, and may that lamp be ever brightly shining! May it be safely kept in the inmost recesses of your soul, sheltered from the winds which blow from all quarters of the horizon! This light is the star on our journey, the lamp of the pilgrim who wanders by night through the forest. There are women who keep alive in their souls a bright, clear, and steady light — the light of great deeds, of generous alms, of holy thoughts. There are others, on the contrary, whose lamp has long gone out, and I will not name to you the places where the divine light of their souls has been extinguished. There are women whose character and conversation have always somewhat of nobility of sentiment and freshness of feeling; they are not of the number of learned women, but after a few moments intercourse with them we feel that their minds and hearts dwell by choice on the summits of the moral and intellectual world; we feel that faith and Christian piety have watered the plant which produces the flowers of their life, and have endowed it with an aspect at once gracious and noble. There are others, on the contrary, who waste their whole powers on the petty details of cooking and washing, or, which is much worse, on all the town rumors, the ill-natured gossip, the train of narrow minded, spiteful littleness, which not only lowers the tone of the mind, but also steeps it in gall and bitterness. Between these two categories of women, my choice is quickly made. I wish you all to belong to the first class; all to raise on high the light of your life, your ideas, your feelings, and never to allow it to sink into the mire of maliciousness and littleness. I would rather see you good, simple housewives, with ideas in accordance with that position, for you may be excellent women without possessing a highly cultivated intellect; and it is far better to be a simple housewife than a spiteful or vicious woman. But what I prefer above all is a woman whose lamp of virtue, intellect, and elevated sentiments is ever trimmed and bright. "Her lamp shall not be put out in the night."

"The valiant woman hath put out her hand to strong things, and her fingers have taken hold of the spindle." To put out our hands to strong things; is not this the business of our whole lives? Man's life does not mean sleeping on a bed of roses; it is a rough and rude path, where he must continually put out his hand to overcome obstacles and difficulties. Let us first consult the history of your own hearts. You have often need to put forth your hand to the repair of damages done in your own souls; you must put out your hand, and put it out with vigor, to arrest that evil tendency of your heart, that impetuous nature, that violent temper; to repress that malevolence, that project of revenge, that bitterness which everywhere betrays itself in your actions, your words, and even in your silence. Your soul is a vessel tossed about in every direction by countless waves; for when nothing external agitates it, a whole legion of blustering winds rise in the interior, menacing it with a violent expulsion. Put forth your hand then, now to the right, now to the left. This constant intervention is most necessary to maintain its equilibrium; and were you the Giant Briareus, to whom fables give a hundred arms, you would always find enough to do. "She hath put out her hand to strong things." See those trying circumstances in which your family may be placed; that rock on which its honor and prosperity may go to pieces; slumber not, be prudent and wise; act promptly and energetically; one single vigorous blow given in time may save all. "She hath put out her hand to strong things." Your house may seem to be magnificent, sumptuous, and, relatively speaking, even luxurious, but in truth it is falling to decay within, and you become aware of it. Set yourself to work, arm yourself with courage; now is the moment when you must put out your hand to strong things, and all the more so because this must be done under the veil of a silence, which is little flattering to self-love, but very favorable to the growth of true and solid virtue. Remodel your house, beginning from below; struggle against a current which you see is injurious; restore regularity where disorder has been reigning; repress the covetousness of others, and thus you will be able to reestablish the foundations of your house. "She hath put out her hand to strong things." If some great misfortune should fall on you and yours, be more than ever mindful of the words of Scripture; put forth not only your hand, but your whole mind and heart also, to all that is hard and difficult. Bear the shocks, withstand the blows of misfortune; be the support of those around you in all their weakness, all their shortcomings; become like the mast of the ship which sustains all — cordage, sails, even the sailors who ascend aloft. "She hath put out her hand to strong things."

What more shall I say? Is there a day in her life in which a woman is not obliged to put out her hand to something? Is not the fair vessel of her family and its affairs exposed to daily piracies and dangers? Is she not called on at each moment to refit the disabled vessel? Then when all seems happily accomplished, there remains to be borne the monotonous round of the self-same duties; the same leaden sky weighs us down without our always even knowing the cause, and the whirl of life ends by making us sick at heart. O Christian woman! Put out your hand constantly to strong things; gird on the armor of patience, humility, and resignation; life is so ordained, you cannot change it. Trial is the inalienable heritage of human existence; you cannot escape it. It will seek you out even on your couch, like the inflowing tide, and you must arise and learn to understand at last the necessity of fighting and of putting forth a vigorous hand to the things of this life. "She hath put out her hand to strong things."

"Her fingers hath taken hold of the spindle." Were I to take this sentence according to the letter, I should expose myself to the repetition, at least in part, of what I already said in my discourse on manual labor; let us, therefore, see if these words are not susceptible of some other meaning.

Fable teaches that the Fates were three goddesses, holding, one, a spindle; another, a distaff; and the third, a pair of shears. They spun the thread of human life, then cut it off; and men's destiny was either happy or unhappy, according to the texture of the wool employed by these inexorable deities. Might it not be said that here below we play, more or less, the part of the Fates? It is we ourselves who, in some degree, mold our own destinies. Some trials and misfortunes must undoubtedly attend us whatever be the texture of the wool employed; despite our prudence, benevolence, and desire for good, we shall not escape contradictions, hatred, petty spirit, lies, and underhand persecutions. Let us take up our portion bravely, as our Saviour and His saints have gone by the same path; let us learn to walk therein courageously, and if not joyfully, at least with resignation. But how will it be, if to the inevitable trials of this life you add pangs and misfortunes brought on by your own vices, imprudences, folly, and ill conduct? Would it not be indiscreet to make you remark that the thread on your distaff was bad? Tell me what is the cause of this wretched self-deception? You yourself. You have conducted a certain business unreasonably, perhaps even in bad faith; you have paid too much attention to self-love, vanity, and purely worldly motives; you desired a brilliant future; you sought only earthly happiness and the deceitful glory of this world. Behold the wool which you spun! Are you astonished at the thread which you find on the distaff? When the Fates spun white wool, said the ancients, life was long and happy; but when the wool was black, then life was filled with misfortunes and disappointments. Oh, you who accuse your destiny! To me it seems that the wool you wove in youth was black and of a bad quality. Do what you will, the stuff of your lives will never be conformable to your desires. And yet I am wrong; with God's aid there is always time to take up a new thread, to infuse excellent wool into the web of life, and to obtain a perfect production from the distaff; but great courage is needed to stop short; to cut away all that is black, and weave anew the tissue of life with spotless white from the fleece of the Immaculate Lamb — that is to say, with virtue, prudence, justice, and holiness, for of such is the wool which covereth Christ — *Lanam Agni Immaculati*.[1]

We may also say that the spindle, the hand, and the distaff represent human life. The wool is an image of all which forms the web of our lives. See how the tissue is torn into fragments;

[1] Ven. Bede, *De Muliere Forti*, t. ii. p. 1046, edit. Migné.

it is seized on by the rapid hand of time, and all must perish. Everything rolls on around us, nothing stays, all is carried away by a force that nothing can arrest; only the thread on our distaff remains; I mean our good works, our virtues, our pious thoughts, our holy actions.

May your lives, my children, be woven with the wool of the Immaculate Lamb! When you shall enter into heaven, the angels will salute those hands with respect, and will exclaim — Blessed be hands which wielded the distaff with such holy skill, and wrought for you beforehand a robe of glory through all eternity. "Her fingers have taken hold of the spindle."

Twelfth Discourse
The Valiant Woman is magnanimous. She loves the poor, and visits the sick.

She hath opened her hand to the needy, and stretched out her hands to the poor. (Prov. 31:20)

MY CHILDREN,
In the explanation of the last two verses from Proverbs on the valiant woman, we saw that it was lawful for her to rejoice in the good that is done around her, and in the success of her undertakings, and to let her heart freely expand at the view of the happiness and prosperity of her family; provided only that her joy was not tainted by pride, and was restrained within the bounds of moderation: For the abuse of even what is best may excite in the soul those feelings of puerile self-love and wretched vanity, so universal among mankind, that one often knows not what advice to give them. If they be told to rejoice in God, to rejoice in all that is good and fortunate in their lives, because the very sight of good dilates and cheers the heart, they let themselves fall at once into all the folly and unreasonableness of a paltry vanity. If, on the contrary, the motives of praise and right appreciation of things be altogether suppressed, and the legitimate satisfaction which necessarily accompanies virtue, according to the doctrine of Saint Thomas, be thus destroyed, the soul pines away, and is

exposed to the danger of losing all energy and activity in doing good. We therefore recommend very great caution in the manifestation of good deeds and the joy taken in them. Setting aside even the motive of humility, our pride, jealousy, easily wounded vanity, and the petty self-loves which, like so many tiny serpents, are ever winding around our hearts, should determine us on living in obscurity, on hiding our happiness and successes, and on moving through this world as much as possible like the quiet streamlet under drooping leaves. After giving an anagogical sense to the next sentence of the Sacred Book — "Her lamp shall not be put out in the night," — and applying it to those admirable women in whose hearts and minds the lamp of holy desires, noble thoughts, and generous feelings is ever kept burning, we pointed out with Holy Writ how necessary it was for woman to put forth her hand to strong things, to arm herself with courage, and to struggle valiantly against the difficulties of life. And, finally, speaking of the distaff in the hands of the valiant woman, we said that this distaff represented life, and that our existence was happy or unhappy, according to the kind of wool we spun.

The following verse may be thus translated, in conformity with the original text — "The valiant woman hath opened her hand to the needy, and stretched forth her arms and hands to the poor." It is not a treatise on almsgiving which I purpose delivering today; that subject would carry me too far, but perhaps on some future day I may return to it. I wish now to consider alms in their connection with the valiant woman, and with the end of our association.

Let us first remember that there exists a strict and rigorous obligation on all of us to give alms according to our means; that there exists for the rich man (and the greater number have that relative wealth which allows of their giving something) an express command to give at least a portion of his superfluity to the poor. The rich man is not, in the eyes of faith, such an absolute proprietor of his own fortune as to be able to use or abuse it at will. No, the rich man, by the justice of God, is but

Twelfth Discourse

a sort of steward, who must render an account to the Great Master of the universe of the treasures confided to him; and one of their chief uses, after a suitable and prudent reserve for his own needs, is, that their superfluity should be poured into the bosom of the poor. But (and on this point I lay great stress, for it is the difference between Catholic teaching and doctrines subversive of all society) the poor man, if neglected, is not thereby allowed to take justice into his own hands. The rich man is not citable before a revolutionary tribunal for his non-fulfillment of the precept of almsgiving: God alone has the right to constitute Himself the avenger of His forgotten poor. This admirable doctrine preserves to the giving of alms its most beautiful quality, that of voluntary action; yet prodigies of charity have been everywhere wrought by its means. Follow any other principle, and you will necessarily fall back into the fathomless abysses of socialistic theories.

Return heartfelt thanks, my children, to Divine providence, which has organized for you this association of charity, and thus given you a means of accomplishing more easily a duty which is binding on all Christians. When we are alone, isolated, without any exterior stimulus, we end by falling asleep over our obligations; we forget, we become careless. Without knowing it, we are slipping down an imperceptible slope, and we shall soon arrive at complete supineness. Such a woman would be charitable, for she is a Christian, good, and naturally kind-hearted, but she never thinks of it. Absorbed in her own home, she meets less frequent occasions of giving alms; the obligation is seldom recalled to her mind and, consequently the feeling of charity perishes within her: She becomes hard towards the poor, not by calculation, but from habit. It seems to me, my children, that, on the contrary, our monthly gatherings, your private meetings, the visiting of the poor, and the whole proceedings of your society are a sermon in action which reminds you of one of your principal duties. You have to hear in every varied form, the waking summons of the indolent and slothful soul, the petition of the poor, and his cry of distress. It is therefore, my children, a special blessing from God that He has called you to form part of this charitable work, which, by uniting together your ideas and efforts, infuses into them a force and power we can never find in isolated attempts. It is a blessing from God, for the graces of heaven are promised to two or three persons joined together in the name of Christ. In this respect, we have nothing but acts of thanksgiving to make to Divine Providence. Our society has increased beyond all expectation; it has developed itself admirably both as to the number of its members and their good qualities; so that today it is not on two or three only that the eye of God rests with complacency, but on a numerous and picked assemblage. There is, then, truly a blessing from heaven on our work. And is not the touching sight of so many pious souls meeting together to assist at the Holy Sacrifice of the Mass, to listen to the word of God, and to concert together on the means to be taken for doing and perfecting good works another blessing from heaven? Yes, my children, I say it feelingly, it is a special grace which has been granted you; and through gratitude and careful avoidance of neglect, which would be highly culpable, you ought to profit by it to reanimate your zeal and your charity in the cause of the poor. "The valiant woman hath opened her hand to the needy, she hath stretched forth her hands and her arms towards the poor." Have you done for the poor and for this association all that you could do? Do not think I am going to frighten you with unheard of obligations. Commence by subtracting from your income all that is necessary and really needed, not only for your absolute requirements, but also for the prosperity and suitable appearance of your household; keep up the position in society which you ought to hold, and let it be maintained with all propriety and graciousness; and in making these concessions, I believe I leave as large a margin as your position, the good name of your family, and your children's future require. But these allowances made, we must return to the first question: Have you done for the poor and our association all that you could do?

Twelfth Discourse

In the first place, as to material help, our subscription is very small indeed, as it was not a maximum we wished to lay down, but rather a minimum, which should be within the reach of every purse; a minimum which may be exceeded, and which we shall always be happy to see exceeded wherever it is possible. Can you not then give more; and if you can, why do you not do so? If you wish that your alms should be in secret, there are a thousand ways of keeping to yourselves the benefit of anonymous charity, and the happiness of having it known only to God. Outside our special association, do you seek to relieve, according to your means, the innumerable forms of misery around?

You will perhaps say — I cannot; the sacrifice is an impossible one; I should only ruin my husband and children in turn. If it be really impossible, I will not insist further; I will even withdraw my question. But is it quite certain that you cannot? Permit me to make an inspection of your wardrobe with you. I do not fear to follow the example of the Fathers in their familiar instructions, and to descend into details which may seem frivolous, but which possess the inestimable advantage of entering into the very heart of the question. What a collection of useless things! How many dozen dresses, shawls, bonnets, and many other objects besides, of which I do not even know the names! Tell me, I beg of you, and tell me honestly, would you not be as well and suitably dressed; would not your appearance in society be quite sufficiently brilliant, were you to retrench one-half at least of that heaped-up pile of things? Who has not met during his life with one or more specimens of those rich ladies, who have got nothing at all? Stop, I am wrong; they possess a number of unpaid bills at every shop in town. They have a mania for perpetually buying everything new — bonnets, dresses, shawls, lace; the latest fashion is ever the best. They have a fabulous number of gowns, and each novelty once bought is worn two or three times at most; then they open a drawer and lay therein the garment, now out of favor, and condemned never again to see the light of day. They

The Valiant Woman

thus contrive to amass heaps on heaps of finery; and if they should be ever obliged to change their abode, the public ought to stand at their windows to see the train of vans go by. I am not exaggerating, my children; I am stating facts. . . . Possibly, you will reply; but in that case there is some monomania, and, thank goodness, I! . . . May I be allowed to observe there are various degrees of fever. Now tell me frankly whether you yourself have not this very monomania, though not at all to the same degree — not to this ridiculous point? Count up fairly all the objects of luxury in your possession; make a tour of your rooms and your wardrobes. How many useless, utterly useless things? — for I cannot term necessary the caprices of a moment, the unreasonable whims of an imagination always in search of new fashions, always ingenious in creating imaginary wants, and which never knows how to restrain itself within the limits of reason, wisdom, or becoming appearances. . . . But let us leave the past and turn to the future. I have a prayer to make to you in the name of our Lord, in the name of the poor, in the name of your own dearest interests and those of your family. Retrench, henceforth, from your bills all really useless items; impose this sacrifice on the requisitions of your whims. Be strict on this point, for, you may be certain of it beforehand, pretexts will not fail you. How many times will not your imagination whisper on entering a shop — how well that dress would become me! What an exquisite effect it would have! And that bonnet, how elegant it is! What delicate tints in those colors! How pretty it would look at my fêtes! And that charming piece of furniture, if I could only buy it to ornament my boudoir! . . . If you listen to this siren's voice, I pity the poor, I pity your husband's purse, and your own folly.

You think you will be happier for the possession of what you covet. You are wrong; and perhaps experience has already enlightened you on this subject. No, you will be none the happier; you will scarcely have had that dress on, that pretty piece of furniture put into its place, when all its éclat will have vanished, all the freshness of its acquisition be faded, while in your heart will still remain a void, and even, if you be a true Christian, the sting of remorse. Yes, of remorse; for is it not true that many women bear upon their persons objects perfectly needless for the requirements of their position, and even for the due splendor of their rank, and which would suffice to maintain many families now perishing of hunger? When things have arrived at this point, it is a certainty in the eyes of reason and faith, that the misery of the hapless poor is as a cry of vengeance against those who commit such excesses. You have heard of violent catastrophes destroying the most apparently well established fortunes, or of those inward sufferings from which the highest station is not exempt, and by which souls are crucified on a painful Calvary, amidst all the magnificence of a brilliant position. You do not know how to explain such unaccountable events. The only true explanation is in the doctrine I am this moment unfolding. Perhaps in such families there existed excesses in luxury and pleasure, which equalled those of which we read among pagans — a sumptuousness almost oriental in furniture and viands, while in the streets were to be found famished, squalid poor, without clothes or food. "And he feasted sumptuously every day. And there was a certain beggar, named Lazarus, who lay at his gate. . ."[1] God waited patiently for a long time, but the hour arrived at last, and His justice flamed forth. He has struck one of those awful blows which are a warning for all. And when He does not punish in this world, it is often but a sign that His anger has reached its highest point, and that He reserves these crimes for the chastisements of the other life, to which the afflictions of this earth are but shadows; for when God strikes us here below, there is always some hidden mercy in the blow. On the other hand, how great the happiness we experience in a sacrifice made for the sake of the poor! And I do not even mean a real sacrifice always, for in many cases it is a mere whim which is in question. You have denied yourself

[1] St. Luke 16:19, 20.

that caprice, and have clipped the wings of that feminine curiosity, which wishes not only to see, but also to possess everything it sees. Is it not to such curiosity that the words of Holy Scripture may be applied — "The eye is not filled with seeing, neither is the ear filled with hearing?"[1] And again — "I will go and abound with delights, and enjoy good things."[2] You have, then, had the courage to practice self-denial, and instead of gratifying some selfish whim, you devoted the money it would have cost to the furthering of some good work, and above all to the relief of the poor. You should therefore deem yourself a thousand times happier; for in the first place, you have fulfilled a precept, and that of itself gives happiness. But we also see how marvelously the Lord has arranged everything: You have done a good deed to the poor, and its remembrance brings sweetness to your heart, and sheds a pleasant perfume on your way. Never will the acquisition of some coveted object, nor the purchase or wearing of exquisite gowns procure for you the joy and peace, the sweet and profound emotion, which the remembrance of a poor man relieved from his misery will do. I thank God for having established such a law, for having so ennobled our minds as not to permit us to find any true satisfaction in the petty frivolity of luxury and vanity. I thank Him for having decreed that our souls can never descend into inferior regions in search of guilty pleasures, without meeting therein bitterness, and sharp stings, and agonizing pains; I thank Him for it, because these misfortunes are often necessary to make man's soul soar upwards to regain that place which it should never have left.

You have done some good to the poor! Do you know what transformation was thereby wrought? It was not to the poor, it was to yourself that you showed mercy. That little coin thrown into the lap of the poor is money put out to interest, money which will be returned to you a hundredfold, and which will obtain for you and your family the greatest abundance of

[1] Eccles. 1:8.
[2] Eccles. 2:1.

Twelfth Discourse

graces. Our God is so generous, that when we give alms for His sake, he does not allow it to be gratuitously done; He constitutes Himself immediately the security for the poor; He bids the angels of heaven take note of the sums spent, that the capital may be returned to us with usury.[1] Some day we shall be much astonished to find what treasures we have amassed in heaven, whose first origin will have been a small alms given with much love, as a tiny snowball on a high mountain becomes the centre of an immense avalanche, which descends and covers whole meadows below.

Do you know why such a family prospers? Look near and you will see the shadow of a pious woman, who, half hidden in the twilight of humility, does good deeds, and thus becomes the foundation on which the prosperity of her house rests. God has not, in the New Law, made earthly happiness the end and chief recompense of the observance of His commandments; yet nevertheless, say the Doctors of the Church, happiness here below usually attends on virtue regulated by prudence.

Now besides happiness, temporal prosperity and even an increase of fortune are among the results which flow from almsgiving; and though this may appear a contradiction, yet it is a truth taught by experience, the more water we draw from a well within certain limits, the more there is to draw; and in the same way, by some unknown mystery of the moral law, it happens that the alms bestowed on the poor often become to the donors a source of prosperity and aggrandizement. One might say that alms resemble the moisture which the sun draws up out of marshes and streams; it is apparently a loss they suffer from the star of

---

[1] "During my solitude of today I could find nothing better to do than to look over old papers and old souvenirs, my own writings and my old ideas about everything. I found some good ones, that is to say, some that are probable; some pious, some exaggerated, and some silly, as — 'If I dared I would ask God why I am in the world? What am I doing here? What have I to do? I know not. My days pass uselessly, neither do I regret them. If I could only do some good, to myself, or another, were it but for a minute each day!' Ah! me, what was easier? I had but to take a glass of water and give it to the poor." — *Journal de Mdlle. Eugénie de Guérin*, pp. 77, 78.

day, yet in reality it is not so, for the water ascending on high changes into clouds, and descends again to them fresher and purer than before. Try it, my children, and you will no longer have any doubt on the subject. On the other hand, how many catastrophes and losses of fortune have been gradually brought on by hard-heartedness towards the poor? And even should no external failure take place, fearful mysteries of retribution are at work beneath the surface. The Lord takes from certain rich people the power of being happy; He crucifies them by means of their own wealth; He scourges them with every object they seem to possess; He commands the roses of their garden to bear nothing but thorns to wound them, till all which ought to render them happy is turned into a source of painful illusions and cruel disappointments. But God, says the Holy Scripture, "hath heard the desire of the poor;"[1] and that desire — what is it if not the happiness of the man who has been his benefactor? I have the utmost confidence in the prayer of the poor when offered for those who have been good to them; in the cry of the wretched for him who has comforted him; and I will not conceal from you that one of the greatest joys I have experienced since my entrance into the diocese has been the following: Some months ago I received a note from a poor girl, whom I had formerly confirmed on her sick bed; I had to walk a few hundred yards to her house. I mention this detail because in that pure soul everything became a subject for gratitude. She was writing me some few simple, touching words of thanks, and concluded thus —"Never, for the last five years, has a day passed without my praying for you." This little sentence did me more good than if the poor child had bestowed on me the most valuable gift. And you too, my children, may procure for yourselves that consolation; you unwittingly do obtain it every day; for I am very sure that there rises in your behalf and that of your families, from many a bed of pain, from many an obscure refuge, an all-powerful cry, a daily supplication, which draws down on you the most precious graces, wards off the gravest perils, and assures your future and that of your children. The Lord

[1] Ps. 9:17.

Twelfth Discourse

has promised it, His word is pledged to it: "God," says the Wise Man, "will hear the prayer of the poor;"[1] and the Psalmist elsewhere adds — "The Lord hath heard the desire of the poor."[2] Alms are, then, but a loan made to God in the person of His poor; money put out on interest and yielding a hundredfold, the repayment of which begins even in this world.

After these general reflections on almsgiving, I return now to a more particular study of our text — The valiant woman "hath opened her hand to the needy, and stretched out her hands to the poor."

The true way of putting this lesson into practice is by visiting the poor, which you are urged to do by the rules of your association, and only then can you truly say that you have extended your arms to the poor. Visiting the poor is one of the chief aims of our society. Do you perform it regularly? Do you not sometimes excuse yourself from it on insufficient grounds? If your occupations are really incompatible with such visits, I do not insist on them; but are your reasons grave ones? Is it not rather a certain indolence, or if you prefer to call it so, a certain timidity of character, which shrinks from trying anything unknown? Or is it a dread of any inconvenience? Fear of having to make sacrifices? I am very far from saying that visiting the poor has not its disagreeables: You must often meet very unpleasant people and things; you must often find yourself face to face with facts well calculated to force you to withdraw in disgust; you may even receive abusive words and injurious deeds as the sole reward of your services. But, my children, are we to suffer nothing for our Lord's sake? Must we not suffer in doing good? We have more merit, and our recompense will be greater. Is not Calvary the Christian's mountain, and is it not better that our sufferings in its ascent should be for justice sake? Besides, you will also meet with some grateful hearts to console you: You will meet — I am sure have already met with many beautiful souls and feeling hearts under a perhaps rough

---

[1] Ecclus. 4:6.
[2] Ps. 9:17.

exterior. The human heart has chords not always touched in vain; and foremost among them comes the sense of gratitude and a remembrance of benefits received. The blossoms of the soul do not, perhaps, spring up at the moment we wish to pluck them. You will meet with natures in which the bud seems altogether dead, yet at some moment when you think not it will astonish you by its unexpected luxuriance.

The sight of poverty has another great advantage; it brings you face to face with suffering — real suffering. You have often complained of things which would rejoice the heart of a poor man; and the cause of your grief is often, at least in part, due to your own imagination, your own whims and caprices, and even to the very abundance guaranteed by a position which renders you more than exacting. Go and look at real suffering; go and contemplate the poor and sickly in their wretched garrets; go and visit those miserable women whose whole lives are but a slow martyrdom, and whose exterior deprivations are nothing in comparison with the desolation of their hearts. Go and contemplate sights such as these, and you will return almost ashamed of yourself; you will return strong, generous, and well disposed to bear your cross courageously in the future. If visiting the poor were productive of no other result for you, that alone would be an immense advantage. You have often spent a great deal of money in going to theatres, whence you brought back nothing but fatigue, emptiness, and a more profound dissatisfaction with yourself. Whilst the sight of virtue in poverty, and a prey to the attacks of infirmity and indigence, will attach you more closely to all your duties, and give you a double consolation — the consolation of a heart which bestows comfort, and that of a heart which compares your lot with theirs. "It is better," says the Wise Man, "to go to the house of mourning, than to the house of feasting."[1] The first gives us a healthy moral impression, while the second too often leaves a void in the soul or a weight on the heart, even though you escape the pangs of remorse, making you pay dearly for pleasures too often dangerous.

[1] Eccles. 7:3.

Twelfth Discourse

I conjure you then, my children — and I address myself to all those among you to whom it is possible — I conjure you to take up again your visits to the poor, if you have abandoned them; or if you have not practiced them, go this very day and have your names inscribed on the list of the Lady Visitors. I beseech you in the most urgent manner to do so, and in no way can you give more pleasure to your Father in Christ than by following this counsel. Visiting the poor is one of the special marks of our society, and I am most anxious to have it religiously adhered to. In going to see the poor in their own houses, you will do good in a way which could not be effected by giving money to other people to take to them, even though the sum might be a much more considerable one. You will see the poor yourselves, and the sight of you will do them good; you will speak to them tenderly, and your kind words will be even more welcome and more efficacious than your alms, or at least, joined to the material help, they will augment its value ten-fold.[1]

---

[1] "As I was going to Cahuzac, I wished to see a poor sick woman who lives beyond the Vère. It is the woman of the rose-tree tale, which I think I have already told you. Good God! what misery! On entering I saw a truckle bed, from which an almost dying head was raised. Still she recognized me. I wished to go nearer to speak to her; but lo! a pool of mud and filth around the bed, caused by the rain dropping through the roof, and by a spring which filtered through the earth under her wretched bed. It was all infection, misery, mouldering rags, and vermin. To have to live in such a spot! Poor creature! She was without fire, or bread, or water to drink, and lying on a heap of hemp and some potatoes, to preserve them from the frost. A woman who had accompanied us removed her from this dunghill; another brought in some fagots, and we made a fire. We then placed her on a bench, and as I was tired, I sat down beside her on the fagots which remained. I talked to her of the good God: nothing is so easy as to make one's self understood by the poor and unhappy, when one speaks to them of Heaven. In their heart is nothing to hinder their comprehension, and therefore it is so easy to console them and make them resigned to die! The ineffable peace of their souls is a thing to envy! This poor sick woman was happy; and what so astonishing as to find happiness with such misery, and in such a dwelling. It was a hundred times worse than a pigsty. I could not find a clean spot whereon to put my shawl, and as it was in my way on my shoulders, I threw it on the branches of a willow which stood in front of the door. And even there it was filthy." — *Journal de Mdlle. Eugènie de Guérin* pp. 109, 110.

THE VALIANT WOMAN

A woman, when she wishes, has at her command those delicate attentions, that gentle forethought, those kindly words which calm pain and help to an increase of strength and patience. It is in visiting the poor she can more especially be a messenger of "glad tidings;" she can suggest salutary counsels with a holy dexterity; she can say some little word, one little word, but say it from her heart, say it with the tone, the accent, the sweetness belonging to her nature: and that one word may, perhaps, half convert a soul, or at least become the germ of its approaching conversion. "The feet of the saints can do great things in the houses they enter," says Saint Chrysostom; "they sanctify the very stones on which they tread; they bring great treasures with them; they correct vicious natures and put to flight bodily evils."[1]

Yes, my children, go visit the poor; be not satisfied with yourselves those weeks when you have failed to do so; you do not know what good you effect; if you had only a glimmering of it, I dare to think that, with the exception of those amongst you to whom it is really impossible, you would all hasten to inscribe your names amongst those who visit our Lord in the persons of His poor. It is in these visits especially that you open hand and heart, and stretch them forth towards the needy.

In a recent journey I saw,[2] intended as a symbol of one of the most beautiful of the Pyrenees valleys, the statue of a woman of graceful form scattering flowers on her way. Let that be the symbol of your lives also; scatter alms, benefits, kind words, and good counsels as you pass; let your hands and hearts be ever open. If money fail you, give the heart's coin; for despite what is said in these practical days, that coin has still its value, and is often more precious than money; it cannot entirely replace money, but it should always accompany the gift of it. And when the limits imposed on the best of wills no longer allow of the bestowal of gold or silver, the valiant

[1] *Eclog. de Eleemosyn.* t. xii. p. 782.
[2] A Bagnères de Luchon.

Twelfth Discourse

woman finds in the inexhaustible treasures of her heart unknown resources, which she freely pours forth with all the tenderness of charity; and therefore it can ever be said with truth of her that — "She hath opened her hand to the needy, and stretched out her hands to the poor."

THIRTEENTH DISCOURSE
Duties of the Valiant Woman, the guardian of the domestic hearth. . .

She shall not fear for her house in the cold of snow: for all her domestics are clothed with double garments. She hath made for herself clothing of tapestry: fine linen and purple is her covering. (Prov. 31:21, 22)

MY CHILDREN,

One of the principal ends of our association is to aid the poor morally and physically, and the most efficacious way of becoming acquainted with their wants and coming to their relief is by visiting them one's self; by mounting those narrow stairs, trodden each day by the feet of indigence; by penetrating into those obscure garrets where misery hides itself, and carrying thereto the healing balm of alms and kind words. Therefore, did I eagerly profit by the scriptural text which seemed to present itself for the purpose of recalling to your minds the chief obligations of our society: "The valiant woman hath opened her hand to the needy, and stretched forth her hand to the poor." Almsgiving is of strict obligation, and an obligation binding on the consciences of all Christians according to their means. Every one, almost without exception, can and ought to give. "If thou have little," says Tobias, "take care even so to bestow willingly a little."[1] Every one has some small superfluity, and can bestow an

[1] Tob. 4:9.

alms with what he spares from the gratification of some whim. After an enumeration of the chief advantages of almsgiving, I insisted strongly on the duty of visiting the poor, specially recommending it to your consideration, and earnestly imploring you to put aside all excuses for not complying with this form of charity. By going yourself to the poor, you can do them a great good; by taking it yourself to the poor, you give double worth to your alms. For is not the mere presence of a kindly disposed person a great benefit in itself, which, when added to material succors, much augments their value? Then those sweet and tenderly compassionate words, those pitying glances on the hardships of the poor, that benevolence which of its own accord seeks out suffering in order to relieve it — all these contribute to render visiting the poor a specially useful and meritorious work, and a work which nothing else can replace. I do not hesitate to affirm that a few pieces of money given in this way to the poor, accompanied by that charity which inspires such devotion, are of more value, and do more good, than will a far more considerable sum which is carelessly sent them by the hands of a stranger. "The valiant woman," continues the Holy Ghost, "will not fear for her house in the cold of snow: for all her domestics are clothed with double garments. She hath made for herself clothing of tapestry: fine linen and purple is her covering."

The commencement of this text shows us how a well regulated piety knows how to unite the practice of the highest piety with an active foresight for all temporal wants and interests. The house of the valiant woman should be a model of order, good government, and of at least a relative abundance. Everything should be "double," according to the expression used by the Wise Man; and as governing means foreseeing, the valiant woman will always have a reserve for unexpected occurrences. Furniture, clothing, linen, dinner services — nothing, in a word, is neglected; everything is in its place, well kept, and in sufficient quantities for all emergencies. The

Thirteenth Discourse

requirements of the different seasons are calculated for beforehand, and precautions taken to make the best of the advantages and disadvantages which each one brings in its train: Winter finds good store of fuel; and summer, well organized plans for tempering the excessive heats; light, cool garments are laid by for the dog-days, and woollen stuffs, well lined and wadded, await the rigors of the frost. "She shall not fear for her house in the cold of snow: for all her domestics have double garments."

Religion, properly understood, not only does not oppose itself to this thoughtfulness, solicitude, and foresight, but it even recommends it, and makes of it a strict obligation and a subject of glory for the valiant woman. There is even a special virtue, which Saint Thomas calls magnificence, and which he says consists in the organizing of vast projects, and the dispensing liberally, yet wisely, the outlays required by a large administration.[1] Of course this virtue does not regard all classes in society, but it can always be applicable in some degree, according to people's condition and the state of their fortune. Religion forbids only excess, and excess must always bear a relation to one's position in society. Religion condemns only an unreasonable luxury, disproportionate to the means of a family; and it also always requires that the portion of the poor shall be dispensed with a liberal hand; but these precautions once taken, she is the first to recommend attention to all household affairs and the keeping up of a suitable appearance. It is especially to women that such recommendations are addressed, because a woman is the guardian of the domestic hearth; she should be ever there to watch over the smallest details. The husband applies himself to business and to all outdoor occupations; the wife devotes herself to her household and to all its interior organization; and nature, which adjusts all things well, has specially gifted her for this purpose, endowing her with intelligence and clear-sightedness for small details, and with an aptitude for foreseeing and prudently combining them.

[1] 2a. 2æ. q. 128, q. 134, *passim*.

The Valiant Woman

Therefore, it is not of the man, but of the woman, that it has been said — "She shall not fear for her house in the cold of snow: for all her domestics are clothed with double garments."

These are your duties, ladies, and nothing can dispense you from them. Permit me, then, again to ask you, do you faithfully perform them? Rather have you not grave omissions on this subject wherewith to reproach yourselves? Would it not be an unwelcome step on my part were I to ask to penetrate into the interior of your houses and examine into all their details? Should I find everything in order? Everything provided for beforehand? Should I not somewhere or other discover an almost permanent disorder, and in some households, alas! nothing but negligence and improvidence? When the husband requires some object, he cannot meet with it, or, at all events, it is not in its place; when winter comes, he vainly seeks the clothing suitable to the season; his children's appearance is ordinarily a grave accusation of carelessness on their mother's part; the servants (for they also are a portion of the household) meet with none of the care and attention to which they are entitled in their quality of fellowmen and fellow-Christians; consequently, they soon weary of their place, and when an opportunity offers are only too happy to go and pitch their tents elsewhere.

Examine one by one into all these points, for they are most essential; they form an integral part of your duties. Undoubtedly, to fulfil them with fidelity you will have to do violence to yourself; you will have, perhaps, to struggle against a certain indolence of mind, a certain apathy of character; you must wage a constant war in order to keep your mind always active and steady to its engagements. But our whole life is a warfare; it is but a fight, a glorious combat, whose reward even here below is found in that peace of heart, that interior satisfaction which follows on duties well fulfilled, and in the testimonies of esteem and affection we obtain from all around us. Take any other path, and you will only meet with weariness, worries, contradictions, and that constant anguish which is each instant increased by a terrible and inevitable struggle, —

the struggle occasioned by the disorder of affairs left in arrear, badly done, or in confusion.

These words of Scripture which we have chosen for our text may be also taken in a spiritual sense. Our soul is a dwelling-place, a divine mansion, and this mansion may, and ought to be, beautifully furnished and decorated. The soul is the spouse of Christ; she should possess numerous and rich garments suitable to each change of season and circumstance. These garments of the soul are faith, hope, and charity; these adornments of the mansion are the knowledge of religion, and the practice of the different Christian virtues. The wife and mother of a family is specially charged to acquire and preserve these costly garments, these precious decorations. Have you thought, even a little, on all these details, which play such an important part in family life? A woman, when sincerely pious, can have great influence in a religious point of view; she can establish the spirit of Christianity in her house, if she will but go gently, by degrees, and take all the precautions dictated by an indulgent forbearance. Without creating any disturbance, she can gradually obtain for herself and for those who surround her the virtue of faith, and the rich treasures of hope and charity; she keeps a reserve of these virtues, and when the souls about her are growing cold, she brings them forth after having warmed them at the glowing fire of her own heart. Souls which are unbelieving grow cold more frequently than is thought — more frequently than they let people know. They grow cold in mind and heart; a heat from Heaven can alone warm souls in the desert of this life. The soul which has no faith, or which rather believes itself to have none, is perhaps a husband, or a child arrived at that age when the passions obscure the intelligence and cast doubts on the most certain truths. Observe him attentively, watch closely every impulse of his heart, and it is impossible but that from time to time you will surprise him in moments when everything in life seems distasteful; when men and things, pleasures and honors, have left an icy void behind

The Valiant Woman

them which none can explain, excepting him who has understood that God alone is the center of happiness and peace. Your husband or your child is suffering from the shivering chill of that aguish fever which has attacked him, and you become aware of it; go seek at once in the stores of your heart for some warm garments — by which I mean the thoughts and feelings of a Christian — envelop him softly in those divine truths which have been kindled on the altar of your own heart. You may possibly thus obtain a marvellous result, and that which you so ardently longed for — the return of a beloved soul to religion, its reawakening to the light of truth — will be obtained by those tender cares of love, far more surely than by perpetual sermonizing and impulsive remonstrances in season and out of season; far more surely than by that intemperate zeal which is far more the offspring of nature and ignorance of the true rules for our guidance than it is the child of grace and charity. But in order that you may not be found unprovided, but be able when the occasion offers to effect this desirable result, your own soul must be thoroughly well furnished — its stores of heavenly garments, of precious virtues, of Christian truths must be firmly and solidly established in the depths of your heart. The heart can only give to others out of its own abundance; if it be empty, or possessed of too little for its own requirements, it has nothing left to bestow on others.

I have no wish, my children, to transform you into female preachers; on the contrary, carefully avoid everything savoring of affectation, everything inopportune. Have regard to time and place, watch for your opportunities in accordance with each one's character and wants, prefer waiting to acting too hastily, and God will, I firmly believe, Himself point out to you the moment when the chills of this world have attacked your loved one, and he will, of his own accord, ask to be reanimated. That is the hour of Providence. All will be the more perfectly and surely done for that soul because of your gradual and gentle preparation for the work; his heart will become detached from this world as the ripe fruit detaches itself from the tree, and you will only have to reach out your hand to gather it.

Let not your servants be excluded from this sweet apostleship of the heart; give the care and attention of a mother to their spiritual instruction and the practice of their religious duties. Watch over their conduct with zealous exactitude, but also with kindly consideration.

The Holy Scripture adds — "The valiant woman hath made for herself clothing of tapestry: fine linen, and purple is her covering." How are we to reconcile these words with those of the Gospel, where it is written as a reproach that the wicked rich man was clothed in purple and fine linen.[1] Saint Thomas agrees with Saint Augustine, that it is not the garments which are of importance, but the dispositions and intentions of their wearers. "Because," say these holy Doctors, "every one should dress according to his position in life as others of the same rank do; there is only sin when reasonable limits are exceeded, or when people let themselves be influenced by motives of vanity."[2] "Vice is not in the external things themselves," the Angelic Doctor continues, "but in an immoderate use of them; whence it results that magnificence of attire becomes sinful only when the bounds of a legitimately established custom among persons of the same rank are overstepped, or when people allow themselves to be carried away by the force of such passions as pride and worldly glory."[3] Again, elsewhere, the same Doctor thus expresses himself (excuse these many quotations; they are necessary in an epoch when exaggerated doctrines in some form or

---

[1] "The spirit of darkness reproached Saint Bridget with her over nicety about food and leading too comfortable a life. The Saint's Angel Guardian answered — 'Our Lord cares little what is eaten if it be not unlawfully partaken of: purple and fine linen and the attention bestowed on delicate health will never keep any one from heaven if they only be accompanied with charity and humility.' It is sometimes advisable not to give up the habits acquired in a superior station."
 — Louis de Blois, *Conclave Anim.* t. ii. cap. iii. pp. 323, 324.
[2] *In Matt.* 9
[3] Summa 2a. 2æ. q. 159, a. 1.

other are no longer rare) — "The adorning of the body should be kept within proper limits by authorized custom, by the rank and by the motives of the wearers. If women dress themselves modestly, yet in a manner suitable to their position and dignity, conforming in moderation to the customs of their country, they not only commit no sin thereby, but, on the contrary, perform a virtuous act, which virtuous act is meritorious if accompanied by the grace of God. . . . But there is sin if their attire be more costly than is warranted by their rank in life, or if they are actuated by a reprehensible motive."[1]

In this, therefore, as in everything, there are two excesses to be avoided; we have here again the Strait of Messina with its shoals on the right and on the left hand. Saint Jerome, in his vigorous style, somewhere scourges these excesses. "Beware," he says to a devout lady, "that after having given up seeking to please men by the magnificence and splendor of your attire, a subtle vanity does not lead you to try and attract notice by a want of neatness and cleanliness. . . . Some people put on cowls and sackcloth fresh from the loom, desiring thus to imitate the innocence and simplicity of children, and only succeed in resembling screech owls and bats."[2]

Saint Augustine, and at a later period Saint Thomas also, make the remark that vanity and ambition may be found in connection with rags and filthiness, as well as with pomp and splendor; and they add that such vanity is the more dangerous, because it often deceives us by a false appearance of piety.[3] This abuse is undoubtedly rare; but it has existed, and may still exist, and I must point it out to you, were it only to show you with what enlightened good sense the Fathers of the Church condemned an excess even in what appeared to be right.

But the most usual and widely spread excess is that of luxury, and in our days it has unfortunately run to an enormous extent, particularly among women. Bossuet complained in his

---

[1] *In Isaï, ch. iii.* t. ii. p. 24, edit. Venise.
[2] *Epist. xxii. n. 27*, t. i. p. 413, edit Migné.
[3] *De Serm. Dom.* l. ii. n. 41, t. iii. p. 1566.

Thirteenth Discourse

time of those women who lavished on their own persons the sustenance of many poor, the patrimony of many families.[1] What would that great bishop have said in this our day, when luxury has penetrated into every class of society, when almost every one exceeds the limits prescribed by his position and fortune; when the gown of the wife often figures in the husband's bank book for a fearful amount, and if not found on the pages of the house account, it will be in the ledgers of the shops. And then we have complaints of their having nothing to spare. I should think so! All their superfluous cash, and more besides, is entirely swallowed up by those thousand and one requisites of vanity, by those ever increasing wants, by that feverish restlessness with which each new fashion is followed, in order that the wearer may be able to eclipse others. For those who act on this system there never can be anything to spare, no matter how considerable their fortune may be. But not all the eloquent excuses, or all the specious pretexts of luxury can hinder the rich man from being brought face to face with the terrible anathemas of the Gospel. Not only will his superfluity disappear, but even that which is necessary for him will be also taken away. If in the present day we see so many families in embarrassments, and so much of their apparent splendor resembling those fantastical mansions where outward decorations have alone been attended to, it is to the progress of luxury that we must in great measure attribute it. Were an exact calculation made of the causes which have occasioned the ruin of certain households, it would be easily shown that one of the principal was this reckless expenditure in articles of luxury, in unnecessary furniture, and in useless ornamentations. Put money at the discretion of an imagination wrought on by a feverish thirst for magnificence, and excited by a love of splendor and habits of profusion, and you may be sure that the most gigantic fortune will melt away like water through those ever lavish hands.

---

[1] *Sermon sur la Nativité.*

And what happiness, what advantage do they hope to gain from all this expenditure? As the English tragedian says — This man's soul is in his clothes:[1] Or perhaps it is in his handsome furniture. Providence easily finds how to chastise these sins of prodigality by means which we do not always see: Such a man values esteem, and finds only ridicule; he seeks balm for his heart, and in a thousand petty ways his feelings are wounded. Sometimes the effect produced has not been sufficiently beautiful, and the hoped for smiles and compliments have not been forthcoming; at other times, jealousy has been excited by comparisons made expressly to annoy, and which set down to an inferior place the man who thought to shine in the first rank. And the end of all this vanity is one dull, weary void, and that indescribable disgust for everything which must inevitably be the portion of such a life. Poor human nature! Alas! When wilt thou be brought to understand a truth essential to thy happiness, and to exclaim — No, my being is of too noble a nature to find true contentment in such vanities. I am too deeply imbued with the infinite not to aspire to higher things, and feel that such a narrow horizon was never meant to be my limit.

Saint Francis de Sales has ever shown himself the right guide for discovering a happy medium in all worldly affairs; and we find him speaking on this subject with his usual good sense — "For my part," he says, "I should wish my penitents to be always the best dressed, but, at the same time, the least tricked out or studied, in company; and, as the proverb says, that they should always be distinguished by their grace, dignity, and becoming deportment. Saint Louis says all in a single word by bidding men to dress according to their position in life, so that the wise and good may not say you do too much, nor the young that you do too little; but in case the requirements of the young exceed the bounds of moderation, then you should be guided by the opinions of older and wiser people."[2]

[1] *All's Well that Ends Well*, act ii. scene 5.
[2] Vie dévote, ch. xxv.

Thirteenth Discourse

It would be impossible to give better advice than this, my children. Admire how unexacting true piety is, and how well it accords with the dictates of prudence and good sense. Have the courage to conform to its rules, and you will be doubly a gainer. While guided by the precepts of an enlightened religion, you will avoid the ridicule which oftener attaches itself to such excesses than is believed, and you will thus be spared all those bitter sarcasms behind your back which would otherwise surely follow you, tearing to pieces every detail of your magnificent gown, and offering you up, a tempting bait, to the malevolence of society. You will never fall into those exaggerations of fashion, so unworthy of a Christian woman, whereby the laws of modesty are outraged. You will retain the esteem of the good, and return from each worldly gathering, after having shed around you the perfume of virtue, which you have rendered graceful and attractive, by knowing how to keep within the limits of propriety. You will have deserved the praise thus awarded by the hand of Fénelon — "It is true that what is most to be admired and most rare is a wise, well regulated mind, which avoids extremes, and which, while paying due regard to the usages of society, yet never oversteps the bounds of propriety. True wisdom is shown by taking care that there should be nothing remarkable or eccentric about our dress, furniture, or our equipages. Let them be good enough to escape the criticism of being devoid of taste, indicative of negligence, and disregardful of appearances, but let there be no affectation of pomp or display; and in this way you will prove that you possess good sense and a mind superior to dress, furniture, or equipage; you make use of them, but you will never be a slave to them."[1]

May you all be guided by these counsels of the illustrious bishop of Cambray, and you will then succeed, as far as is possible on earth, in solving a very difficult problem, how to please both God and man —...*dilectus Deo et hominibus*...[2]

---

[1] *Avis à une dame sur l'Education.*
[2] Ecclus. 45:1.

There exists a law which is not always sufficiently thought of — it is the law which governs the relations of our interior and exterior. If a woman has a taste for dress, and indulges it to affectation, she does so to the detriment of her mind; for the more assiduously she cares for her body, the less will she cultivate her intellect. True Christians who ever strive to act rightly, are always suitably and modestly attired; they may be the best dressed of the company, as Saint Francis says; they do not even deny themselves splendor, if their rank or some special circumstances warrant it; but one easily discerns in their appearance that their "soul is not in their clothes," that it soars far above such exterior ornaments, only using them according to the laws of fitness, and ever preserving that noble supremacy of heart, and that liberty of mind which nothing can enchain. It may be truly said of such Christians that their interior is all the more beautiful because of the little importance they attach to the beauty of their exterior.

Fourteenth Discourse
The virtuous wife can polish the manners of a stern husband, however abrasive his character.

Her husband is honorable in the gates, when he sitteth among the senators of the land. She made fine linen, and sold it, and delivered a girdle to the Chanaanite. (Prov. 31:23, 24)

MY CHILDREN,

The house of the valiant woman should be a model of order and neatness. To a woman specially appertains the guardianship of the domestic hearth, the cares of housekeeping, and the duty of foresight for everything concerning the future prospects and welfare of her family. This was the first meaning in which we took these words of Holy Writ: "The valiant woman shall not fear for her house in the cold of snow, for all her domestics are clothed with double garments." Then rising to a more spiritual meaning we found that the soul also should have a provision of divine raiment, which divine raiment is composed of the Christian virtues. Now the soul needs this divine raiment to keep off the cold, both from herself, her family, and all who cry out for help.

The verse which followed led us to lay down the principles of sound theology respecting dress, the ornamenting of the body, and all habits of luxury in general. Under this head two very different errors may be committed; there may be either too much negligence or too much sumptuousness. This latter fault has attained gigantic proportions of late years; the feverish thirst for luxuries has taken possession of every class; the lower vie in prodigality with those above them, and their extravagance is often, relatively speaking, both greater and more common.

We made use of the doctrine laid down by Saint Francis de Sales, that you might hear the dictates of prudence and good sense on this subject. The holy Bishop who tells us "that he wishes his penitents to be among the best dressed people in society," can scarcely be accused of not making sufficiently large concessions both to human nature and to the requirements of society.

The two next verses shall form the subject of the present discourse — "Her husband is honorable in the gates, when he sitteth among the senators of the land. She made fine linen, and sold it, and delivered a girdle to the Chanaanite."

"Her husband is honorable in the gates, when he sitteth among the senators of the land." At first sight it seems as though we might pass over this verse in silence, as in no way applicable to yourselves. Were I preaching at Paris before the wives of senators, then perhaps there might be room for some seasonable counsels, as well as for words of congratulation, but here in a quiet provincial town the text seems at least superfluous. And I fancy I hear you say — Let us proceed to the next verse, for my husband is not one of the illustrious of those great assemblies; he never has sat, and probably never will sit, among the senators of the land. You must permit me, my children, to differ from you on this point; and I mean to endeavor, at least, to strike the letter of our text, as Moses did the rock in the desert, and see if perchance some crystal waters will not flow therefrom. Granted that your husband is neither senator nor deputy, is he not at least a member of some municipal council? No, is your reply, my husband can boast of no dignity whatever; he leads a quiet, retired life. Be it so, but still he is a member of some public body or other; he must

Fourteenth Discourse

occasionally assist at certain meetings, he must go from time to time into the world, for there is a "world" for every class of society. That is sufficient for my purpose, and from it I can take occasion to offer you some salutary advice.

I wish you first to call to mind all that has been said respecting the difference which exists between men and women; on the mutual and beneficial influence which they exert over each other, and on the immense advantages resulting therefrom. Be assured I am far from desiring to depreciate a man of eminent qualities; what I am about to say will not apply in very many instances, at least not entirely; still I do not consider the following observations wholly unnecessary. If a man's influence is often happily exercised over a woman's nature, there is also a reciprocal effect which is perhaps not always sufficiently appreciated.

Endeavor then, my children, that your husband, who is endowed with such admirable qualities, should also show himself not inapt in the thousand and one little delicate circumstances ever arising in life. Exert as much as possible over him that genial influence of good manners, politeness, and elegance which wins its way through the most rugged nature, moulding and fashioning it anew, and in the end imparting to it at least a relative air of grace and polish. Woman possesses a fine perception of many little things which escape a man's notice; she has a faculty for divining a multitude of petty details which, though seemingly insignificant in themselves, yet often exercise a decisive influence in the world. The action of woman's character on man's resembles that of the pumice-stone, which smooths away all roughness and imparts a brilliant polish. It may not always be as successful as it is to be desired; but if a clever and pious woman knows how to use all the advantages which the resources of her heart and mind place at her disposal; if she is never hasty, but ever soft and smooth as oil, it is impossible that she should not succeed in establishing a lasting and salutary influence. It is impossible that this oil so perfumed with love should not unconsciously diffuse itself over her husband's character till all his thoughts and feelings are imbued with it, and he thereby acquires that indescribable suavity of manner and elegance which gives an air of distinction to all his words and actions. There are, undoubtedly, many different degrees in this elegance of manner, but even should you only succeed in laying the foundation of it, you will have always commenced a good work. The first blow of the hammer has its special utility; it is followed by many others, through whose means the statue is finally brought to that degree of perfection of which the artist had dreamt.[1]

I also recommend you always to endeavor to bring your husband's good qualities into notice, while you skillfully throw a veil over his defects: that is the way to raise him in the eyes of others. "Her husband shall be honorable in the gates." Do not imitate those silly women who betray, from want of reflection perhaps, all their family secrets; who proclaim aloud all their husband's faults, that they may thus, at his expense, raise a pedestal for their own petty vanity. Far from concealing they expose, instead of praising they blame, and thence result the most singular rumors, the most embarrassing situations. Every word is repeated, added to, exaggerated, and some charitable tongue is always found to carry back those kind sayings to the husband, who naturally feels hurt, and thus is laid the foundation of a coolness which may prove fatal to affection; and the first line is traced of a breach which goes on ever widening. When, on the contrary, a husband learns all the delicate precautions taken by his wife to increase the estimation in which he is held by others, to throw light on his good qualities and keep his defects in the shade, he cannot but feel deeply touched, and his heart is drawn nearer to her who so well understands the duties of married life.

[1] Saint Chrysostom well describes the influence of woman on man. Nothing escapes the observation of the saints which has any reference to the great human family. "*Nihil fortius muliere religiosa et prudente ad deliniendum virum et informandum ejus animum ad quodcumque voluerit.*" — Quoted by Saint Bonaventure, *Pharetræ*, l. i. cap. viii. t. vii. p. 252.

Fourteenth Discourse

You see then, my children, that there does exist a real and serious application of those words of Scripture to every one of you — "Her husband shall be honorable in the gates, when he sitteth among the senators of the land." Every one cannot be a senator's wife by merely desiring it, but by earnestly wishing it, she can act prudently and perseveringly; she can act like the smooth, calm waves, which, by their constant caresses of the rocks of the shore, communicate to them finally a rounded, polished surface. It is only necessary to carry on the effort slowly but unceasingly, and by degrees the sharp angles become effaced, the character well balanced, and the temper and habits softened and ameliorated. Then, when the time has arrived for taking his seat in the municipal council, for presiding over an assembly of artisans, or merely for assisting at some public meeting, or at some festive assembly, the husband of our valiant woman will be distinguished above all others; on him a special seal seems set; his intelligence is keen and well ordered, his character is full of amenity, his words show forth the well harmonized ideas of a fertile and clear head; the hand of a good and clever woman has been at work, and left its traces everywhere.

Admire, my children, the beauty of Christian wedlock rightly understood! What a beautiful and noble institution! Two beings brought together that their separate moral and intellectual qualities may make a perfect whole. The husband infusing strength, courage, and perseverance into the wife, and covering her with the shield of manly protection; the wife softening all that is too rough and forcible in the husband's character, polishing his manners, giving grace and development to all his interior powers, correcting his tendency to sternness, the harshness of his too hasty decisions. True, you may say, nothing can be more beautiful, but how rarely do we see it realized! Yes, it is a rare sight; but that is all the more reason for my placing it before you as a model for your hearts and understandings, in order to excite you to imitate it at least in part. And even should I only succeed in refreshing your heart by the contemplation of an ideal for poor human nature, there will always be some advantage gained by sketching out these pictures to you. Everything which elevates the mind is beneficial to it, fortifies and consoles it, even though no other practical results may follow from it.

The valiant woman "hath made fine linen and sold it, and delivered a girdle to the Chanaanite."

It may happen that the valiant woman is engaged in commerce, which is what the verse just quoted supposes. In that case, I will give her two most important counsels, in as far as her dependent position permits; they are, strict honesty and a gentle, patient manner.

Strict honesty! In what branch of commerce shall we find it? And yet who wishes to be thought dishonest? Therefore, all sorts of expedients have been suggested, frauds are veiled, disguised, kept out of sight. To an upright, simple conscience, it is, in plain language, fraud, a manifest robbery, because a positive deception is practiced; but in the world it is termed commercial cleverness. The vine would be much astonished could it know what is sometimes sold as its produce, and even when a large proportion of the wine is the pure juice of the grape, still there is sure to be a mixture of different qualities, and, above all, a deceitful brand attached to the bottle. This man adulterates his flour, that other weaves inferior materials with the texture of his silks, linens, and woolen stuffs. It is true that a certain license is permitted to trade; the application of artificial means to the raw material is not forbidden, if restrained within due limits; but it is on the condition that the nature of the articles should not be by degrees absolutely altered, so that the buyers are shamefully deceived either as to the value or the quality of what they buy. Then one must give up trading! I am far from drawing such a conclusion: I say, on the contrary, men should remain in commerce, setting therein an example of scrupulous integrity, by the practice of which they will obtain universal respect, amass a reasonable fortune, keep a tranquil conscience, and draw down the blessings of

Providence on their house and family. I defy the most skillfully well-combined frauds to produce the same results. "Deceitful weights are an abomination before the Lord,"[1] says the Holy Ghost. These are strong words, no doubt; still they are true. Be yourselves the judges: your family is numerous; among your many children should some employ their cleverness in deceiving their brothers and sisters, in laying snares for them, in depriving them of their share of the common inheritance — would you not be highly indignant? Our God is the great Father of all; and can you expect that He will not look with an angry eye on those unnatural children who deceive the members of the great human family, and make use of their superior intelligence and wider experience to possess themselves unjustly of their money; not by actually putting their hands into their pockets (that would be a dreadful crime! they'll say), but by persuading them that such a thing is good when in reality it is either very bad, or at least very inferior for the price asked; or by passing off some unwholesome beverage for the pure, unadulterated juice of the grape. There is, perhaps, some difference, but it is to the credit of him who openly robs his neighbor of his purse, for he at least acts openly. Therefore is fraud, in the Holy Scriptures, everywhere severely condemned, and the strongest terms of reprobation used against it. And truly the curse of God does often seem to fall heaviest on the family of the fraudulent dealer. He appears to succeed at first; but his prosperity is transitory; small chinks show themselves in his vessel, they gradually enlarge, and the ship soon sinks forever. Even when he does permanently prosper and acquire considerable wealth, still does the hand of providence chastise him in his children and those dearest to his heart. Like the poisonous exhalations which in a single night cover whole forests and marshy places, pain and grief suddenly arise in those smiling, fertile plains, and penetrating into the interior of the household, leave behind them sadness and despair. Read the Scriptures; its menaces are terrible: but

[1] Prov. 11:1.

did we know the secret history of some families, we should find they are oftener carried into effect than we at all imagine. "He that gathereth treasures by a lying tongue is vain and foolish: and shall stumble upon the snares of death. The robberies of the wicked shall be their downfall, because they would not do judgment."[1] And again elsewhere — "The riches of the unjust shall be dried up like a river: and shall pass away with a noise like a great thunder in rain."[2]

But let us suppose that everything does succeed, externally, with the clever man whose conscience is not over scrupulous about his dealings; then attend to a mysterious decree of Almighty justice, to which we have many times partially alluded, but on which, on this occasion, I lay particular stress. Our happiness is not derived from external things, but from the nature and reality of the enjoyment we find in them. It is not enough that flowers are growing in your garden when you wish to obtain honey, you must also have bees who know how to extract it from them; wasps make a great noise, but they cannot elaborate the precious juices. And thus does God deprive the rich man of that faculty whereby the just soul extracts from the things of this world the greatest amount of legitimate happiness which Providence permits. In place of honey, they too often have to drink a bitter draught which poisons their whole life. This may seem incredible, yet it is an oft repeated story and if we could but get at certain confidences, hear the recital of some men's secret histories, we should then understand what anxiety, pain, and disappointment unlawfully acquired wealth brings to its possessor. It is in the secret recesses of men's hearts that God daily holds His tribunal of justice and stern retribution, and it may be truly said that the judgments of the Lord commence even in this world.

Adepts pretend that in some cases of magnetism, the person under its influence, when holding in her hand a glass filled with a certain liquid, and drinking of it, cannot distinguish

[1] Prov. 21:6, 7.
[2] Ecclus. 40:13.

the flavor of the contents of the vase, but tastes instead a different flavor which has been determined beforehand by the will of the magnetizer. However this may be, I only use it as an illustration of how God, the great magnetizer of all beings, makes use of such a magnetic influence in the mysteries of His justice or of His tender goodness. You see some persons placed in the most trying circumstances of body or mind, and who according to every law of nature ought to be dreadfully unhappy. Consider them attentively; they are under the influence of a magnetic charm, of a divine nectar; it is true they hold in their hands a bitter potion; but it is not that they drink. They taste only a delicious draught, to which I know not what name to give; a draught whose flavor is determined by the Divine will, and may be called in turns peace, confidence, resignation, and love. O my God, how good art Thou to Thy servants, even whilst appearing to chastise them! Thou puttest to their lips the bitter cup of suffering, and that which seemed a poison restores to life; that which ought to destroy fortifies and reanimates. In this guise truly, O Lord, Thou deceivest Thy children. Thou deceivest as a Father and a Friend; Thou deceivest with the tenderness of a mother. "To whom hath the root of Wisdom been revealed: and who hath known her wise counsels?"[1]

On the other hand, look at the rich man, the spoiled child of fortune. He possesses everything to make him happy — wealth, dignities, pleasure, position in society — and yet he is wretched, thoroughly wretched. When his sufferings are not actually acute, he is oppressed; he seeks to breathe freely, but cannot. Here again is an individual magnetized by providence, but in a contrary sense to the other: he raises to his lips the cup of earthly happiness, and the hand of God, partly in vengeance, partly in mercy, has infused therein a poison to disturb and agitate the inmost depths of his being. Nothing gives him satisfaction; and the last stage of his malady is a sovereign disgust for the things of this world. So true

[1] Ecclus. 1:6.

is it that externals do not make us happy; but the amount of enjoyment which we succeed in extracting from them is the sense of happiness; and this sense, in its true acceptation, is a divine gift, which our Lord gives or withholds according to our merit or unworthiness.

"The bread of lying is sweet to a man," says the Holy Ghost, "but afterwards his mouth shall be filled with gravel."[1] The style of Holy Writ has at times something indescribably picturesque and energetic in its comparisons. Have you ever trodden paths strewn with rough gravel? How difficult it is to walk on it! With every step forwards, you step backwards at the same time; your feet become wearied with these never-ceasing efforts, and you long with all your hearts for smooth and level ground. Then how could you bear this same gravel in your mouth? You shudder at the very idea of such a torture, and your teeth are set on edge at the mere mention of it. This is precisely the simile used by Scripture to explain the anxieties, the weariness, the preoccupation, and the torments of the man who eats the bread of lying — that is to say, who accumulates riches unjustly. He chews gravel only, and it were better far for him to eat black bread moistened with water.

The first essential, then, for the valiant woman engaged in commerce is probity. This strict honesty in business will never hinder her from making reasonable profits, from laying by a provision for her children's future, or from daily adding to her income; but this success in the material prosperity of her family, this increase of fortune, will be effected honorably and honestly; it will be the fruit of honest, conscientious labors, and the reward of a usefully spent life. The bread eaten under these conditions is always sweet to the taste; it never turns to ashes under the teeth, because it has been gained by truth and honest labor.

The second quality which I recommend is a gracious manner joined to much patience. Affability is a very important, but very difficult, virtue to preserve unaltered, especially in

[1] Prov. 20:17.

Fourteenth Discourse

some circumstances. Men usually judge very hastily and from superficial appearances; sometimes one slight passing act of no very serious importance draws down upon us a decided judgment, and a judgment the more scrupulously exact in proportion as it is one of condemnation. We might say that the public had its hand always uplifted to strike, but rarely to absolve. A man of little worth in reality will be lauded to the skies because he has a pleasing manner, and on some occasion or other had been ready with false, flattering phrases of courtesy; while the most thoroughly amiable character, the kindest heart, the most upright man, will be pitilessly scourged for a momentary ill humor. Such is the way of the world, and we cannot change it; it is wiser to accommodate ourselves in some sense to its requirements, and we have the more reason to do so because affability is a virtue. Be, then, always courteous towards the persons who frequent your house; if they do not buy anything, at least let them take away with them kind, pleasant words; it will be the best means, and a perfectly lawful one, of increasing the number of your customers. One often prefers paying a little dearer and having before one a smiling, agreeable face. If, on the contrary, you present a sour, disagreeable countenance, you will alienate every one.

This is, then, a counsel of much importance, but it is very difficult to follow sometimes. One of the chief trials of public servants is this necessity for being always collected before a considerable number of persons constantly succeeding one another. There is a real, serious effort, only learnt by experience, and little appreciated by many people, in receiving others always with a gentle, serene, and equable manner. One often meets characters excellent of their kind, but they seem to magnetize you with an antipathetical fluid, and should, unfortunately, silliness and self-sufficiency be joined to this fluid, a real persecution is the consequence; the poor victim is on the rack, and needs a firmness and a resolution out of the common to preserve his accustomed serenity. This can only be done by untiring efforts and a complete control over one's self;

and the most powerful lever to produce this result is true interior piety, which detaches a man from self-will and keeps his mind evenly balanced by means of a divine force.

May these few counsels implant peace more and more in your families; may they aid the development of your worldly interests, increase the legitimate growth of your fortunes, and draw down upon your households, "the dew of heaven and the fat of the earth, . . ."[1] that is to say, that twofold blessing which sanctifies a family, and assures its prosperity and happiness even here below on earth.

---

[1] Gen. 27:28.

Fifteenth Discourse
True beauty: a veil of glory that radiates the exterior of the woman who has the invisible elegance of a virtuous heart.

Strength and beauty are her clothing: and she shall laugh in the latter day. She hath opened her mouth to wisdom, and the law of clemency is on her tongue. (Prov. 31:25, 26)

MY CHILDREN,

We have the habit of commencing these discourses by a *résumé* of the foregoing one — a plan which has perhaps the double advantage of linking together the heads of the doctrine, and of recalling to memory what has been said at our last meeting.

The valiant woman should endeavor to refine and polish her husband's character by the gentle contact of her finer nature; to soften his disposition by communicating to him some of that exquisite penetration, that delicate perception of little *minutiæ* which is of so much importance in social relations. This is one of woman's noblest and most admirable missions, and when she knows how to accomplish it, she can much enhance the value of what would otherwise have been a wild, uncultivated vine. Therefore, we gave that explanation of these words — "The husband of the valiant woman is honorable in the gates, when he sitteth among the senators of the land." And though the post of senator can only fall to the lot of a few privileged persons, yet the valiant woman can always put in practice, in some degree, these counsels of the Holy Spirit, and by her means, her husband may acquire a certain distinction which will enable him to take his place in a suitable manner in the assemblies of the wise and prudent elders, for such is the original meaning of the word "senator."

The verse which followed furnished us with an opportunity for giving some practical advice to persons engaged in commerce. We particularly recommended to them probity and courteousness: probity which should direct all honest trading, and which is the parent of solid and lasting prosperity — the only prosperity an upright man and a Christian should ambition; and courteousness which attracts customers, and is one of the surest and best means of succeeding in business.

The next text shall be the subject of today's commentary — "Strength and beauty are her clothing, and she shall laugh in the latter day. She hath opened her mouth to wisdom, and the law of clemency is on her tongue."

"Strength and beauty are her clothing." In demeanor, figure, face, and looks, the valiant woman displays a dignity full of charms. It is not an effeminate beauty addressing itself to the senses only, but a ray from heaven whose exterior loveliness is but as the outer husk or covering of a noble and steadfast virtue. She goes on her way wearing around her this veil of glory, and there is so much simplicity in her manners, so much goodness in her words and smiles, such an elevated expression in her physiognomy, that all jealousy is disarmed, and one can but admire and love her. "The root of this beauty," says Saint Ambrose, "is an ever-living interior piety, and the flower projects itself over her whole being."[1] The sight of this admirable woman elevates our thoughts in place of debasing them, and the light of her looks sheds purity around her. When beholding her we recall that beautiful saying of Saint Clement of Alexandria — "He who looks on beauty with a pure affection forgets the loveliness of the body in that

---

[1] *De Offic.* l. i. cap. xlv. n. 219, t. iii. p. 89, edit. Migné.

Fifteenth Discourse

of the soul; he gives to the body the same admiration he would to an exquisite statue, and rises by means of that earthly beauty to the great artist, and to the very essence of all loveliness. These exterior forms are for him a sacred symbol, which he points out to the angels who guard the paths to heaven; that beauty is the luminous seal of righteousness, the sweet odor of a soul in perfect harmony, the manifestation of the inmost feelings of a heart inspired by the Holy Ghost."[1]

Behold the true beauty of a valiant woman; it is like a fresh spring welling up in a virtuous heart; like limpid waters which reflect the rays of an interior sun, and which seem to refresh all who look on them. Her powers are upheld by grace, and grace is protected by the bulwarks of a divine power. "Strength and beauty are her clothing." All these admirable qualities, whose source is ever from within, may be met with in women who do not possess what is styled physical beauty of feature. There are persons to whom the world awards, at least in words, the prize of beauty, yet who, to a close observer, have a decidedly disagreeable expression. Their mind betrays itself in certain fleeting lines, certain wrinkles which come and go, producing an effect which the pen cannot render, but which the understanding seizes on their rapid passage. On the other hand, we often meet with faces which some people would call ugly, yet which are really beautiful in expression and spirituality. True beauty, that which emanates from the soul, is imprinted on their countenances, and shines forth like a splendid diamond not richly set, but which seems to display all the more brilliancy because of that very want. When contemplating them, the words of another holy father, from whom we have already more than once quoted, rise to memory — "Virtue, like a beautiful flower, shows forth on the bodies it animates, investing them with a pure and gentle radiance."[2]

---

[1] *Stromat.* l. iv. cap. xiii. p. 1326, edit. Migné.
[2] Clem. Alex. *Pédag.* l. ii. cap. xii. p. 543.

I have not hesitated to enter into all these details in order to make you understand more and more clearly that religion is an all-preserving aroma, even of the most fragile, sometimes of the most dangerous qualities which a woman possesses. Christianity is strong enough to speak out boldly even on the most delicate matters. It is strong enough to guard all, because it is divine. Whatever your external appearance may be, ladies, act so that the reflection of a noble and virtuous mind may always be visible on your countenances. If God has endowed you with bodily advantages, let virtue be the root from which they derive their nourishment; they will then have more freshness and lasting power, like the trees which send their fibres deep into the earth to draw forth sap, but which dry up and perish should their roots be only on the surface. If nature has not gifted you as highly as you might have wished, let your virtue shine still more brightly, and this blossom of the soul, as the saints term it, will shed around you a yet more brilliant light, because of the simple casket which contains it. A bouquet of flowers has sometimes an additional charm when the vase which holds them is not of the first elegance in design. In this fallen world there often exists a startling contrast between the outward form and the wealth of the mind, and everything is surer and more to be relied on when the material element does not predominate.

Let, then, strength and beauty be your clothing. At church, on the promenade, in the drawing-room, let your countenance be the mirror of all one loves to imagine existing in the heart of a virtuous woman; let your smile have the charm of interior sweetness; let your looks be the portrayed epitome of your feelings; let your bearing have the dignity and simplicity of a truthful soul — in a word, let everything about you command respect, render virtue attractive to others, and elevate the tone of their minds.

The Scripture adds, that "the valiant woman shall laugh in the latter day." One of the most beautiful and touching sights is to see the mother of a family surrounded by the children and grandchildren whom she has brought up in the fear of God, whom she has watched growing and prospering about her, like the evergreen shoots of the olive.[1] Her heart expands, her face is radiant with smiles; she is like to the setting sun sinking to rest in a clear sky, which, before disappearing behind the horizon, seems to delay its course, and regard with complacency the beautiful world it has vivified. "And she shall laugh in the latter day." She recalls with delight the happiness she felt when first she became a mother, the blessings which heaven was pleased to shed upon her family, the tranquil enjoyment of her husband and her children. The labors which she undertook, the pains she suffered, the sorrows inseparable from the happiness of this world, the anxieties and preoccupations of her affection — all are now for her a subject of gladness. She is happy; she rejoices like the gardener who finds in the remembrance of his hard work and constant sweat a subject of consolation, because in autumn he will reap abundant fruits from those days of toil and pain. Happy mother, rejoice, then, in the good you have wrought! rejoice over it in God; for such a joy is a gift from Him. Let the happiness, the virtue, the prosperity of your numerous family be for you a crown of flowers, a green bower wherewith to shade and adorn those latter days of your pilgrimage, and to embalm your wearied limbs, before they descend into the tomb, to find there eternal repose. "And she shall laugh in the latter day."

But it is, above all, at her last hour and on her bed of death that this bright smile of the valiant woman wears its most angelic expression. She is, without doubt, obliged to say with the holy Patriarch — "The days of my pilgrimage are few and evil,"[2] for that law is binding on all mankind; but the tears drawn forth by pain and sacrifice are the most efficacious dew for the spiritual growth of the soul. But after this avowal, which truth demands, the valiant woman can add — "O my God! I have finished my course, I have done the work which

---
[1] Ps. 127:3.
[2] Gen. 47:9.

Thou gavest me to do, and now I return to Thee, O Father, from whom all paternity is named, that I may love Thee better, and supplicate Thee with more earnestness and fervor for those I have left behind me." Then the priest responds — "Go forth, Christian soul, out of this world, for thy Saviour is ready to receive thee into the flowery plains of Heaven." The soul at these words rises up and wings her flight on high; and when she has departed, there remains behind on lips and eyes and brow a calm, angelic smile, which seems the last farewell of the spirit, lingering there to give an assurance of her eternal bliss. "And she shall laugh in the latter day."

Let us now look at the opposite picture. We will sketch it briefly, that you may not be over-saddened. See yonder woman of the world, who has never thought of life in its serious aspect. Her youth has been passed in a round of pleasure and excitement, amid all the amusements of this world. She has neglected the care of her household; she has not sought to keep her husband's love by those amiable qualities which are the best safeguards of a lasting affection. She has neglected her children's education, leaving them to the care of other persons, in whose selection even she never stopped to exercise judgment and reflection. She did not watch over her household, and by degrees disorder, in every form, introduced itself therein; illusions have vanished, old age has arrived, seductive pleasures have disappeared, and the reign of stern, bitter realities has commenced. She ends by finding herself left alone in life, like an aged, withered tree. She looks around, but all is gone, save the sad phantoms of her own recollections; her heart is steeped in bitterness, and tears only are left her in her solitude. . . . Poor, unhappy soul! Let me come to your aid and show that all is not yet lost, if you will but follow my earnest counsel. Now is the hour to return to your God, for God is so good, that with Him there is no "too late." Pray to Him with love and repentance, and He will send down on your heart that refreshing dew wherewith He consoles and comforts the afflicted; that withered heart will revive under its influence, the thorns which pierce it will be drawn out, and once plunged in this celestial bath, it will grow green again. Water it daily with tears of compunction and hope, and these tears, mingled with that dew from on high, will obtain for you a new life, and you will cry to God in accents trembling with love and gratitude — "This old trunk has not yet lost all hope, though its roots had grown old in the earth and its stem seemed to be lying dead in the dust, yet at the first contact with water it has grown green again, and clothed itself anew with foliage as in the days when it was first planted:

"'At the scent of water it shall spring, and bring forth leaves, as when it was first planted.'"[1]

"She hath opened her mouth to wisdom, and the law of clemency is on her tongue." Silence and reserve are among the qualities most to be desired in the valiant woman, because women very often fail in them. Some years ago three of our discourses were devoted to sins of the tongue, so I do not intend to speak again in detail upon them. I will only say a few words to explain this sentence of the Wise Man — "She hath opened her mouth to wisdom." How many persons there are who daily open theirs to folly, anger, revenge, calumny, and impurity! Let there be found, here and there, at least, some truly Christian women who have placed the key of their lips in the keeping of wisdom — of wisdom, in the choice of their words, never saying aught unbecoming or unworthy of a religious soul, and ever respecting authority, belief, morality, and the laws of society; of wisdom in being sparing of words; think before you speak, and do not publish your thoughts with the precipitation of a frivolous mind. A few words spoken with good sense and prudence have more effect than the interminable conversations of those superficial minds who say everything because they know nothing. Few words and many good actions; that is the right way to do good and to acquire the reputation of a wise and upright mind which knows how to restrain itself within due limits. Your wisdom must also

[1] Job 14:9.

show itself in the choice of time and place for speaking. Expressing a certain opinion may be harmless one day, and the next be like throwing oil on flames. Suppose the conversation to turn on some question or other, when your opinion is asked, give it frankly yet prudently, and your reply is sure to have a good effect. If, on the contrary, you yourself originate the conversation, you will have the appearance of showing off, of having studied your phrases beforehand, and you will only bore your audience, and set them against you. On this point there are a variety of imperceptible shades we must know how to seize on and comprehend. There must be tact, reserve, and reflection; tact, to observe the direction of the wind; reserve, in order to study it fully; and reflection, to follow its course judiciously. Let there be also wisdom in your choice of persons. You find yourself in a select circle of safe and tried friends; how many things may you not say innocently there which would be like applying fire to powder if uttered before others. And why so? Because those now listening to you are prudent, well meaning people, who understand the true bearing of your words, the limits to which your thoughts extend, and they will stop short of those exaggerations by which it is so easy to distort an idea that is quite right and good in itself. But if these same words which flow freely from the heart in conversation with intimate friends, without being weighed and measured by a geometrical rule, were uttered before prejudiced, unintelligent, evil-disposed persons — before narrow minds, warped by malevolence — do you know what results would follow? The very meaning you never intended to give will be that attributed to your conversation; that which you had formally rejected will be set forth as the true expression of your thoughts, although you requested that the sense of your words should not be distorted, but kept within the limits of reason and truth. The innocent candor of your speech will be poisoned by some noxious viper who has insinuated himself near you unperceived to prepare his darts against you; he will infuse venom into your best thoughts, into your

Fifteenth Discourse

most inoffensive projects, and you will receive ere long by the post of public rumor a second edition of yourself — not a true edition, but one maliciously added to, travestied, and falsified. You will scarcely have a right to complain of this. Why did you let the beams of your inmost life fall on those twisted, streaked, and lumpish panes of glass which we term false hearts and malevolent minds? You must not be astonished if the aim of your thoughts and the form of your words have been quite wrongly represented, for that is according to the nature of the minds who have been listening to them. Ah! My children, let me conjure you before opening your mouths, go to the door, and see first whether it is Wisdom who knocks; if it be really she who commands, then all is right: open instantly, open freely. Speak out boldly, and God will bless what comes from your heart. But be careful too; for within us are many sirens who sometimes counterfeit the voice and language of wisdom. These sirens are various in kind and manifold in number; they are called intemperate speech, love of gadding abroad — that is, of going forth or forsaking the interior home of our heart — vengeance, anger, love of detraction and calumny — in a word, the unruliness of that member which the Apostle calls "a restless evil."[1] Watch over yourselves then, my children, with the utmost care; pause before you speak, and if you doubt, be silent. These precautions are the more necessary because self, with all its good qualities, is a little weak on this point, if we may believe moralists. Here is a portrait sketched by one of the most celebrated commentators of the Bible *à propos* of this verse — "There are women who are idle, curious, and unceasing talkers; they are devoid of all steadiness, and constantly agitated by the gusts of passion. Therefore they are often guilty of many imprudent, malicious, and impertinent speeches."[2] I quote this passage, though well satisfied it does not apply to any of you; but it is sometimes good to explain morality by pointing out extremes.

[1] St. James 3:8.
[2] Cornelius à Lapide, in *Prov. 31.*

Lastly, the Scripture says — "The law of clemency is on her tongue." What an admirable sentence! The lips of the valiant woman are the depositories of the law of clemency. To man is assigned strength, courage, and somewhat of sternness in the government of his family. I do not mean to condemn this sternness, for it is necessary, and without it a family would fall to pieces from excessive indulgence; but it will not do alone, and what is wanting will be found in the heart and on the lips of the wife. When a husband has made himself heard in those tones of authority which infuse life and energy into every department, then comes the wife and touches with the oil of sweetness all the springs and wheels, smooths away all friction, and facilitates the execution of his commands. If the father maintains towards his children that firmness which is a sure guarantee of success, the wife is ever there to guard against too hasty measures, to tone them down, to add gentleness to them, without depriving them of any of their strength. To the energetic words of the father she joins a mother's counsel, a loving word, an affectionate glance, and this wise combination of gentleness and force makes all go on smoothly in the household. The Wise Man has somewhere said, and we have already quoted his words, that conflicting tendencies and powers are to be found in all the works of God. This idea, which is the explanation of so many contradictions, is also applicable to a family. There exists, and there ought to exist, in a husband and wife different capabilities and varying manners of action which lead to the same end, but by ways apparently opposed to each other. Unfortunately, married people do not sufficiently understand this marvellous doctrine; the wife reproaches her husband with severity, the husband in his turn complains of his wife's weakness, and the words are bandied from one to the other as reproaches. In place of thus retorting recriminations, would it not be better to blend the wife's gentleness with the husband's firmness? In this union they would both find exactly what they were seeking for, yet which they are now themselves destroying by a foolish separation. Let the husband keep on his lips the dictates of firmness, and the wife the law of clemency on hers, and these two principles of action, blended together by a mutual affection, will make the happiness and assure the prosperity of their family.

Another meaning also may be given to these words — "The law of clemency is on her tongue." "The valiant woman," says the commentator already quoted, "is neither morose, nor caustic, nor dissatisfied, but is sweet, gentle, modest, and benevolent."[1] What a painful sight is malevolence, and yet how common! How rare is benevolence, and yet how exquisite and precious a quality! It is not only most admirable, it is also most conformable to truth. What tongues of vipers do we not meet with in this world![2] What a love of wounding and annoying others! You may be sure that it is not a law of clemency which is on their lips, but a law of malice, perfidy, and calumny. But you, my children, must seek to be of the number of valiant women, such as the Holy Spirit describes them. Lay down for yourselves a law of benevolence, charity, kind interpretations, and gentle words. How far happier and more peaceful will you then feel! When a serpent in human shape retires into her den, she suffers acutely, and the recollection of the venom she has shed about banishes all rest; but a calm and happy life, and peaceful slumbers are the portion of those Christian souls who show respect for the persons and feelings of others, who diffuse only kindly words around them, and who, even on the brink of an abyss, prefer to fling flowers rather than stones.

By following these maxims you will attract universal consideration, and all will recognize and confide in your goodness of heart. Your memory will be ". . .like the composition of a sweet smell made by the art of a perfumer. Your remembrance

---

1 Cornelius á Lapide, in *Prov. 31.*
2 Father Faber speaks of some persons in whom "devotion only develops a capacity for criticism, and excites their sensibility till it becomes quite morbid."
— *Conferences,* pp. 27 1, 272

shall be sweet as honey in every mouth, and as music at a banquet of wine."[1] If, on the contrary, you take pleasure in attacking the memory of others, your own reputation will soon suffer. Everyone will say, after hearing you talk of your neighbor, "All the day long thy tongue hath devised injustice; as a sharp razor thou hast wrought deceit."[2] How keen is its edge when exercised on others! Probably my own turn will soon come, and I, too, shall pass under the teeth of the saw![3] When people have once earned this reputation for themselves, they may, perhaps, be well received and flattered to their face, because they inspire fear; but scarcely is their back turned, when all such forced politeness vanishes, and many a weapon is unsheathed to cut their character to pieces. It is the law of retribution, "Eye for eye, tooth for tooth;"[4] and though men may be, and often are, unjust in applying this law, yet Divine providence often makes use of the malice of men to accomplish the work of its own all-seeing and all righteous justice. Then does the guilty one experience in his turn the sad truth of those words of Saint Chrysostom — "There is nothing worse than the tongue; it is more dangerous than snares, more cruel than a sword."[5]

Therefore, my children, let the law of clemency be on your lips and in your words. If this great commandment of charity were observed by all, what a blessing for society, what an increase of sincerity in men's relations with each other! Join to it that law of wisdom which Holy Writ also recommends to the valiant woman, and then you will merit in its full sense that commendation of the Holy Ghost — "She hath opened her mouth to wisdom, and the law of clemency is on her tongue."

---

[1] Ecclus. 49:1,2.
[2] Ps. 51:4.
[3] *Ibid.*
[4] Lev. 24:20.
[5] *Fragmenta, in Job v. Supplem.* t. xiii. p. 590, edit. Migné.

Sixteenth Discourse

God has entrusted these children to *you* and they live in *your* house. The Valiant Woman knows her children well and cares for every aspect of their lives. Nothing escapes her notice.

She hath looked well to the paths of her house, and hath not eaten her bread idle. Her children rose up and called her blessed: her husband, and he praised her. (Prov. 31:27, 28)

MY CHILDREN,

Strength of character tempered by sweetness, and a dignity of manner full of charms, are the clothing of the valiant woman. Her beauty emanates from the soul, it commands respect and inspires noble and generous sentiments. There is nothing effeminate or voluptuous in it; virtue is depicted on every feature, and attracts only to raise on high. Therefore, she never has to suffer those bitter pangs reserved for women whose frivolity and good looks have been the cause of lamentable falls. Her old age is surrounded with respect and affection, and on her death-bed the happy smile of a soul predestined to bliss is on her lips. "And she shall laugh in the latter day."

The Holy Ghost adds, "She hath opened her mouth to wisdom, and the law of clemency is on her tongue." We drew occasion from this text for many counsels with regard to conversation, to a due reserve in speech, to a wise choice of fitting times and opportunities for offering advice and reproof, and

The Valiant Woman

we earnestly dwelt on the necessity of moderation and prudence in words: advice so often given and so constantly forgotten in practice. Finally, my children, we represented you as clement and compassionate rulers, ever showing an example of sweetness and tenderness in your families, always voting for peace, causing the scales of justice to lean towards the side of pardon, and in all your dealings with men in general, seeking to excite in them that benevolent feeling which is ever disposed to excuse and justify.

Let us now continue our discourses, which are rapidly drawing to a close. "The valiant woman hath looked well to the paths of her house, and hath not eaten her bread idle. Her children rose up and called her blessed: her husband, and he praised her."

"She hath looked well to the paths of her house." We have very often said that the care of the household belongs specially to the wife; to the husband's portion fall all external business, great enterprises, and distant journeys. The wife, like the bird in her nest, sits brooding over her little ones, shielding them from harm by her love and active forethought. Nothing escapes her; and if God has endowed her with a quick penetration not to be duped — if He has gifted her with that clear-sightedness for suspecting and finding out what is sought to be concealed from her eyes, it is because she has a mission from providence — a mission to watch over the home-life of her family, to preserve it from danger, and keep it ever calm and peaceful. Happy the family which thus reposes in the love of a truly pious woman! Happy the nest over which the maternal wings extend themselves for warmth, or around which they flutter and poise, seeking to discover aught that might trouble their children's happiness. That family can repeat with tranquil confidence the words of the Prophet — "And I said: I shall die in my nest, and as a palm tree shall multiply my days."[1]

---

[1] Job 29:18.

Sixteenth Discourse

Have you, my children, done as the Wise Man counsels? Have you looked to the paths of your household? Do you know by whom those paths are trodden, and where they lead? We will enter into some details on this point, if you please. You have servants; do you know them thoroughly? Do you feel perfectly certain of their morality, honesty, and discretion? Do you know what acquaintances they have made, whom they introduce into the house? Have you sufficient guarantees for their good conduct, so as to feel assured on that head? Do you not rather content yourself with those half-assertions, which usually end in the saddest consequences? Remember, I am far from wishing to transform you into official inspectresses, distinguished by all the stiffness of word and manner ascribed to pedagogues. What I want is an active but kind watchfulness — the faculty of seeing everything without being a spy on people's actions; of being able to look about in a simple, unaffected manner. With these conditions, the vigilance of the mistress never becomes a nightmare to her household; it is submitted to unmurmuringly even when a little dreaded; the necessity for it is understood even by those who would willingly evade it.

Do you exercise this constant, daily watchfulness over all those dear to you, including your well-loved little ones? Do you know what places they frequent, with what people they associate? Do you know the nature of the society they select? What am I saying? Do you even know what they are, or what they have become in your own house? Alas! there are, perhaps, many mothers whom these questions will profoundly astonish, because they have never put them to themselves, nor even supposed that there could be any occasion for putting them. Their children, indeed! They rarely think about them, except, perhaps, at meal-times; for one must do them the justice to say they are very careful that it should be known and said that their children are well fed and well cared for, that robust health should display itself on their countenances, and do honor to the good cheer of their table. As for the rest, it is the least of their preoccupations.

Others attach a very great importance to their children's success; but what flatters them most in it is the honor that accrues to themselves, their maternal vanity being so agreeably tickled; but as for the morality, good conduct, or religious feelings of their children, those are cares which have never troubled them; they have plenty besides. Do not think I mean to blame an anxious solicitude about the lawful, reasonable success of your children, or the efforts made to promote it, and advance them in the world, provided the laws of moderation and Christian prudence are not transgressed. But your children's future does not consist solely of these things; and while you accord a suitable share of thought and foresight to these legitimate interests, you should not neglect what is most essential — "These things you ought to have done and not to leave those undone."[1] Watch over your children's education; watch over the culture of their minds; employ all the means at your disposal to insure their success; but do not neglect the culture of their souls. Remember that in the garden of this life one flower is necessary, the blossom of faith; and where that heavenly plant does not flourish, all the rest will quickly fade — above all, true happiness.

Christian women, you can exercise on this point a most powerful influence by your example and counsels, by your goodness and patience, but above all by prayer. It is true, when your child arrives at a certain age, it seems as though his intellect had escaped your control, and the reins of his mind had been withdrawn from your grasp, yet your influence is better grounded and more extensive than it appears to be. Your power over the heart, if you know how to use it wisely, is undying, and your words, if inspired by a mother's love, are like the falling dew, which can always penetrate to the very roots of life, even intellectual life. The heart and soul sway our convictions more than we believe, and if a mother knows how to play on the chords of the heart, all is not lost. A loving glance, an affectionate counsel, a sad and

---

[1] St. Matt. 23:23.

dignified silence, will sometimes work wonders in a soul which has remained unmoved by the most eloquent preaching. The remembrance of Saint Monica, perhaps, did more, after the grace of God, towards effecting Saint Augustine's conversion than any other external means.

To insure beforehand these happy results, you must carefully watch over your child from his earliest age. Watch over his going out and coming in; observe the manner in which his days are spent, for in some unheeded moment he may perhaps be tempted and fall. The spirit of evil is also watching the soul of your child, and has unfortunately an ally in the citadel. This ally is the inherent perversity of human nature, which is often developed with fearful precocity in some children. It is this innate corruption which frustrates the most skilful efforts, and inspires young people with notions which they alone could find out in order to elude the most active vigilance; it is this which teaches them deceit and trickery, and how to gloss them over with an appearance of candor. Take heed especially of the books which your children read: even at the risk of repeating myself, I must insist in the strongest manner on this point. Have the courage and the forethought to keep from their sight all those publications which do so much harm in these our days. If you possess a library, let it be opened with the utmost care and prudence to the youthful members of your family. I am not alluding here to books essentially bad in their principles, for I take it for granted you have none such in your collection. But very often books which are in themselves good, at all events not positively hurtful, may contain a certain amount of danger for your children's hearts. There are beverages which sustain and fortify the man arrived at mature years, which would yet kill the fragile being whose nourishment is still being drawn from its mother's breast. This maxim of ordinary prudence is, however, habitually set aside in the usages of life, and particularly in the education of children; and many a time has hasty, inopportune, and premature knowledge wrought the most frightful ravages in the mind of youth.

THE VALIANT WOMAN

These, my children, are your chief duties in the bringing up of your offspring. In order to fulfil them well, infuse into all your words, acts, and looks that loving, motherly tenderness which easily obtains all it wants, because it combines authority with affection. The more constant and active this watchfulness over a family is, the more it requires to be softened with love and unselfishness, for thus only can that which is very unpalatable to the independent nature of young people be relished, or at least borne with. Remember what you yourself were in early years, and make allowances for the young. Though your opinions and feelings have been modified by age and the experience of life, there is one thing which nothing can alter, and of which riper years only demonstrate more and more the great utility; and that is, benevolence and affection of heart, a condiment always essential to the banquet of life, but most especially so when the food prepared has some taste of bitterness. That this bitterness is necessary I quite agree — it is even indispensable to assure a happy future; but at least let it be tempered by a mixture of suavity and tenderness.

"The valiant woman hath looked well to the paths of her house." The superintendence of children and servants is not all-sufficient. You must also keep your eyes open to everything that happens in your house. Let nothing escape you; let certain goings out and comings in be searched into, and their cause perfectly understood. Learn how to foresee and prevent, and you will find plenty of means of resistance which you see not at present; you will discover innumerable simple proceedings for the quiet frustration of certain intrigues — for a woman can always cut the meshes of the most skillfully woven plans without being detected. But to do this she must superintend everything properly; she must be thoroughly conversant with all the paths leading to her house or issuing from it; she must hover over it as the bird does over its nest; and be able to see clearly even in darkness and perplexity. There must be no scandal, no hasty acts, no imprudent words; but a firm, quiet, gentle rule, which combines the force and the smooth action of the tranquil wave as it throws the boulders back on the beach. It carries them swiftly on to the sand, and its strength is as irresistible as its motion is calm.

I hear indolent minds, quite terrified, exclaim — "What unceasing labors you are preparing for us! what activity you require! what incessant work, what constant, hourly occupation, even when apparently at rest!" It is true, my children, that to put this advice in practice you must not slumber, for if you sleep the enemy will come and sow tares amidst the wheat in the field of your household. To follow these counsels you must ever stand in the breach. But real life is perpetual activity, and this activity is the source of all its order riches, prosperity, and happiness. Idleness, on the other hand, is the mother of all vice and disorder, and of every misfortune. Without activity and labor of body and mind your home will soon resemble a field covered with briars and thorns, and God grant it may not also become the resort of venomous reptiles!

The Wise Man well understood this activity of the valiant woman, for he adds — "She hath not eaten her bread idle." Saint Paul says — "That, if any man will not work, neither let him eat."[1] If these words of the Apostle were rigorously acted on, how many would have to fast daily and absolutely! The valiant woman, on the contrary, does not eat the bread of idleness, because she is always occupied. She rises early, diffuses order around, distributes work to all her people, exciting their energies by her own example, for she loves to work with her own hands, while she is careful not to neglect the culture of her mind. Like a ship laden with rich merchandise, she reenters each evening the harbor of her home, bringing with her precious treasures. If at times she seems inactive, it is only that, like the bee, she has shut herself up in her hive, to prepare some delicious honey — the honey of holy thoughts, of interior reflections, honey culled from the fairest blossoms of her mind and heart. At other times, she is exerting secretly all the powers of her intellect, and her life is spent

[1] 2 Thess. 3:10.

The Valiant Woman

in silent, hidden labors, all the more active and painful that men know nothing of them. But whatever may be the nature of her work, or the sphere of her activity, the valiant woman "never eats the bread of idleness."

How many women are there, on the other hand, whose entire life is idleness, whose days drag wearily on in a state of perpetual indolence! One might say they are always slumbering, like that stupid animal naturalists call the sloth. The only member in constant use is the tongue; and it must be allowed that this member labors incessantly, and does most admirably and completely the work of all the others. One would say the others have made it their administrator, and wishing to repose themselves, have delegated to it the mission of stirring about in their place, and certainly no executor of a last will ever perform his task so perfectly. Nevertheless, the tongue is precisely that member which very often would do better to keep quiet, and whose inopportune use is as hurtful to our own interests as to our neighbor; and it has been justly remarked, that when it is very active it is always to the detriment of everything grave and serious.

Follow the life of that frivolous woman: what does she do from morning until night? Nothing, or almost nothing. Half her day is passed in useless visiting, frivolous conversation, and discourses in which more than one of God's commandments are frequently broken. The rest of her life is a fleeting cloud, a castle in the air; she is ever dreaming, and often on the brink of precipices; her imagination, all on fire, pours itself forth like a stream of lava; her sentimental mind feeds itself on visions and unreal schemes; or, perhaps, she shuts herself in her room, and holds converse with those frivolous and dangerous books whose every page gives forth a pestilential vapor, where poison lurks in imperceptible quantities under every word, and kills the soul by slow degrees. A profound slumber and indolence which absorbed every faculty of mind and body would be even preferable for that misguided woman. At least, such a slumber would be in some respects harmless; but that idle life of dissipation and frivolity, that stupor into which these dreams of the imagination plunge her, sap all morality! It is poison disguised under a seductive form, which soon brings on a seductive lethargy.

The Scripture adds — "The children of the valiant woman have arisen and called her blessed: her husband, and he praised her." What more beautiful and consoling than to see a venerable woman, the mother of a family, surrounded by the esteem, the confidence, and the love of her children and husband? When she moves through her house with graceful, stately bearing, all her family rise up to do her homage, and joyfully point to her, saying, behold our glory, the root of our life and happiness, the centre of our love — that dearly prized centre, where all our hearts meet to be more closely drawn together, more ennobled and purified. Yet more, hers is the spreading shade where we delight to repose and refresh ourselves; and as in former ages the place of rendezvous was always under the old oaks of the forest, so it is also in the ever-youthful heart of the wife and mother that her family hold their meetings, it is there all grows calm and serene, the clouds of life disappear, and cheerfulness is born again of love. Delicious draught of motherly affection, you are necessary in order to procure for us all the bliss of domestic happiness! With you the annoyances of life are forgotten, and the sweet cup you present, joined to the excellent harmony of the feelings you awaken, recalls the words of the Scriptures — "Wine and music rejoice the heart . . . " of man.[1]

There may be, and there often unfortunately are, many clouds, my children, on the horizon of home; characters are so different, passions so many and so complicated in their effects, that undisturbed serenity is impossible. But when a woman has fulfilled her duties well, when she has been a true Christian, when she has ever brought a steady front to all her obligations, with a constancy of purpose, an unwearying tenderness of love, and a long-suffering patience, the hour of jus-

[1] Ecclus. 40:20.

tice and of gratitude must come sooner or later. One day her husband will arise, making a sign to his children, and all will bow down respectfully before her, saluting in her the angel of the domestic hearth, pronouncing her blessed, and conjuring her to open her heart still more, that she may dispense from it the hospitality of an affection ever welcome, and ever seeming to give a new life to her family. There shall spring up a great joy in that mother's heart on that day, and she will rejoice the more fully because of her children's happiness, or rather both sources of joy will blend into one.

The Royal Prophet says — "They that sow in tears shall reap in joy."[1] Is not this sentence the abridgment of a woman's life? She sows in pain, in grief, and in labor; and often cold, frost, and snow, the rigors of winter and the burning heat of summer follow on her sowing. But how rich is her autumn! How sweet the season when she reaps what she has sown, when she gathers in a harvest all the more abundant because of her sufferings! Yes, such is life! We come and go, casting the seed of kind thoughts, words, acts, and benefits; casting into the ground all the best treasures of our soul, and watering them with our tears. "Going they went and wept, casting their seeds. But coming, they shall come with joyfullness, carrying their sheaves."[2] Flow on, ye tears of life, sad drops from the heart, flow abundantly, and sink into that earth which you are to fertilize. Flow on, though she who sheds you suffers bitterly, drawn as you are from the inmost fountains of her heart. Such true tears, saints tell us, are the life-blood of the soul, the drops of anguish wrung from the heart. No matter, flow on, however you be named — the life-blood of the heart, the anguish of the bosom, or the overflow of a soul overwhelmed by grief and painful labors; flow on still, for you alone can yield a real harvest, the harvest of souls; you alone can prepare a treasure of virtue, wisdom, and prosperity.

[1] Ps. 125:5.
[2] Ps. 125:6, 7.

Sixteenth Discourse

Let it be thus with you, my children. May you, too, after much suffering, share one day in those spiritual harvests, in the bosom of your own families; may the hearts of husband and children, like clusters of ripe grapes, be seen to hang around your path inviting you to gather them, while husband and children bend around you like those sheaves of wheat of which the youthful Joseph dreamed, and offer you the homage of their respect, love, and gratitude. "And your sheaves standing about, bowed down before my sheaf."[1]

I cannot terminate this discourse, my children, without in my turn rising to proclaim your filial piety, and to return you a father's thanks for all your kind sympathy and ardent prayers during my recent trials.[2] The answer has been in accordance with your wishes, and today I can literally carry out the words of Scripture, with a slight alteration, and say — "Your bishop rose up and called you blessed."

---

[1] Gen. 37:7.
[2] The bishop had been seriously ill for over a month.

SEVENTEENTH DISCOURSE
A recapitulation of the sixteen discourses: the fruit of valiance...

Many daughters have gathered together riches: thou hast surpassed them all. Favor is deceitful, and beauty is vain: the woman that feareth the Lord, she shall be praised. Give her of the fruit of her hands: and let her works praise her in the gates. (Prov. 31:29-31)

MY CHILDREN,

The valiant woman must consider well the paths of her household, and keep her eyes open on all that passes within and without it. Like a bird, she must hover closely over the nest of her little ones, or fly around it to examine and take all necessary precautions against danger. Children, servants, all persons having access to her house, the thousand details of domestic life, nothing must escape her vigilance. This surveillance should be kind and gentle as well as strict. It will then correct efficaciously, and at the same time temper whatever bitterness may be the result of such warnings and corrections.

A constant activity is necessary to fulfil these duties. Therefore, the Wise Man adds, that "the valiant woman hath not eaten the bread of idleness." Rising early, she brings the day's work into order and directs everything; like the busy bee, she does all the more, because she loves to hide herself in the cells of her home; very different from those idle women who spend their lives in foolish dreams and silly talk, in useless visits, and in reading frivolous books, or even perhaps bad and dangerous ones.

A sweet reward awaits the valiant woman; it is sometimes deferred, but is sure to crown the latter years of her life. Her virtues, long unacknowledged, are at length fully appreciated, and sooner or later her husband and children unite to lavish on her every mark of respect, and proclaim her to be the centre of their love, and the source of their life and happiness — "Her children rose up, and called her blessed: her husband, and he praised her." Then comes a great, deep joy in the heart of that mother and wife; she has sown in tears, she will reap in gladness.

Today, my children, these conferences on the valiant woman, which have been already, perhaps, too long, shall be brought to a close, for we are about to comment on the last verses of the chapter which serve as my text.

"Many daughters have gathered together riches: thou hast surpassed them all."

The commentary on this text obliges us to recapitulate the many admirable qualities of the valiant woman; it will form the bouquet of these instructions.

The valiant woman resembles in her household a vessel laden with rich merchandise; by a wise economy, an intelligent activity, and a knowledge of business, she augments the possessions of her family, and increases the revenues of lands and capital; she combines and foresees everything so thoroughly, that nothing is ever wanting in her house; it is always well stored with provisions, and she fears neither the rigors of the season nor the inclemency of the weather — even on this point we may say that the valiant woman enjoys a marked superiority over all other women. Like Saint Gregory Nazianzen's mother, "she is so occupied with worldly interests that she seems to forget God, and yet so united to Him that she appears to be a stranger to the affairs of this world."[1]

---

[1] Greg. Naz. *Orat. xviii.* cap. viii.

Seventeenth Discourse

But the principal treasure of the valiant woman does not lie here. She has been endowed by heaven with great mental superiority, and by the help of grace she daily augments this precious possession. Her mind is enriched with those acquirements which may be useful in her sex, or are ornamental to it; her heart is a spring ever welling up with pure and noble feelings, with divine affections, with elevated views, and with generous projects; her character is a union of grace and dignity, of gentle amenity and elevation of mind combined with simplicity. Her whole person seems formed of delicate tints, where one contrasting shade only perfects and completes another, and whose whole shows us an exquisite picture of amiable, attractive virtue, chastened by a thoughtful gravity. She resembles the graceful yet powerful vessel which is launched forth on the open sea, fitted with sails and masts, with rudder and a sure pilot. Her voyage is a prosperous one, and when she returns to her port, her family is waiting to receive her on the shore, and salute her with all the love and just feelings of pride, which a mother so perfect and revered ought to inspire.

She is the glory of her husband, and his comfort in affliction; she gathers into her heart the tears he sheds, and transforms them into the dew of affection; she is the fountain from which he draws prudent counsel, and a just appreciation of men and things, and in this respect she supplies what is deficient in man's intelligence. With her delicate tact and keen observation, she discusses the snares which are everywhere hidden, and divines beforehand what it would be perhaps too late to avoid at the actual moment of peril. By her gentle influence of heart and mind, she corrects the asperities of man's character, she smooths down its sharp angles, and imprints on his mind as well as on his manners the stamp of a distinguished bearing, or at least she succeeds in effacing from his disposition all that would lower him in the eyes of the world, or make him disagreeable in his contact with other men. How many have been thus improved and perfected in their intellectual relations, by their daily intimate intercourse with a vir-

The Valiant Woman

tuous woman; who, like a fine delicate stone, rounds and polishes the things it touches. Therefore, in her does the heart of her husband repose all its confidence, and he has no need of other riches; he finds all he requires in the love of his wife, and rests therein in peace. "The heart of her husband trusteth in her, and he hath no need of spoils."

The valiant woman is also for her children the fountain of wise counsel and prudent warnings; she daily seeks to perfect more and more the life she has given them; as a gardener lovingly cultivates and tries to bring to maturity the young plants he has raised in his green-house. She directs the superior parts of their nature heavenwards, and yet lets them take root on earth, that they may one day accomplish the mission which God will appoint for them. She watches over them with tender anxiety and unceasing solicitude; she corrects them affectionately; she prunes away all useless or dangerous shoots, and gives to the sap that regular, prudent course, by which all flaws are avoided. In all difficulties and perplexities, the valiant woman is the stay and support of her family; in misfortunes she puts forth a rare energy, and becomes to them the unshaken rock on the ocean shore, where the wreck of the vessel may be safely piled.

Do you know a valiant woman? Have you the happiness of being reckoned among her intimate friends? What mines of wealth you will daily discover! What veins of gold unseen by vulgar eyes! What goodness of heart! What delicacy of soul! What benevolence and large-mindedness! What patience in little things! What calm, unmoved resignation in all the trials of life! What a mild, steady light is her intellect! How warm her heart! How noble her soul! Yes, if you do know a valiant woman, go often and feast on the flowers of the garden of her mind, and you will return exclaiming that her possessions exceed the possessions of all other women — "Many daughters have gathered together riches: thou hast surpassed them all."

But above all, what treasures will you not discover if you can penetrate into the sanctuary of her soul, that holy, blessed spot, where she seems already to be touching upon Heaven! What a perfume of piety is in that secret oratory! What deep and close communion with her God! There you will see the divine birth of all the good wrought in that predestined soul, which is to diffuse itself later in deeds of religious zeal, maternal devotion, and social benevolence. You are at the chief fountain which waters the garden, which refreshes and brings to perfection all natural good qualities, and bears in it the seed of virtues which nature by itself could never produce. Like that Pyrenean mountain[1] which gives birth to a number of different fountains, prepared by the Creator's hand for the cure of many maladies, the enlightened piety of the valiant woman is to her the source of a thousand different streams in which her entire being is daily steeped and renewed, and which alternately become for her a spring of vital energy, and a source of courage, of gentleness, of wisdom, of love, of intelligence, of calmness, of patience and resignation. Ah! If it is ever given you to know the secrets of that soul, especially the secrets of that inmost portion which is in close communication with the Divinity, with what joy and holy envy you will exclaim: Other women have gathered together riches, but nothing can be compared with the treasures amassed by the valiant woman. "Favor is deceitful, and beauty is vain: the woman that feareth the Lord, she shall be praised," continues the Holy Spirit. As I am most desirous never to depreciate the gifts of the Great Creator, I will repeat here again that beauty in itself is a precious quality, and that it comes from God, just as all that we call goodness, truth, and splendor. "O Lord," cries out Saint Augustine, "Thou who art the Infinite Good and Supreme Beauty, in whom, and by whom, subsist all beauty and goodness."[2] "All earthly loveliness," says another Father, "is an image of God's tenderness for man, and a visible proof of our Creator's bounty."[3] And Saint John

---

[1] At Bagnères de Luchon.
[2] *Soliloq.* l. i. cap. iii. p. 599.
[3] Basil. *Seleuc. Orat. xii.* n. 1, Patrol. Græcq. t. lxxxv. p. 158.

Climacus adds — "Truly it is a marvellous thing to see the pure soul make use of that which to others is an occasion of ruin as a ladder whereby to mount to God."[1]

No one, then, shall have cause to accuse me of depreciating the gifts of God; but in this our fallen state, does not that gift of God which we call beauty often become an occasion of vanity, a stumbling block, a deception, and a danger? Of a certainty, amongst all visible objects there is nothing that so forcibly reveals to us the goodness and beauty of God as the noble character of a woman, the beauty of whose form is but the splendid covering of a virtuous and exalted soul. But how rarely do we look on things from this point of view, and with how much reason has the Wise Man said, "Favor is deceitful, and beauty is vain."

It is vain and deceitful, because in the first place it so soon passes. It is but the blossom of a day, a flower opening at morn, and withered at night. Thence arises in many a fear of growing old, which they look on as an intolerable misfortune, and a sort of daily martyrdom. Roses quickly fade, but they at least know what to do; they no sooner fade, than they drop and disappear. Is it always thus among living roses? To how many of them may not the witty remark of Saint Francis de Sales apply — "Old people who assume the ways of youthful beauty are always laughed at; such folly is only pardonable in the young."[2] Melancholy illusion of life! A young girl is pretty, or believes herself to be so; but after a very few seasons she begins to fade like the roses: she does not perceive it; her mirror, or rather her eyes, deceive her. She grows old: what am I saying, she is already old, as worldlings count. I speak of that apparent external old age which matters little in the eyes of a just soul. And yet she believes herself still in the season of flowers; and when we see her passing along, so naively confident that she still appears young, we are involuntarily reminded of the holy Bishop of Geneva's words — "Favor is

---

[1] *Grad. xv.* pp. 894-991, edit. Migné.
[2] *Introduction to the Devote Life*, ch. iii. p. 25.

Seventeenth Discourse

deceitful, and beauty is vain," because both very often become an occasion of danger. In the state of original justice and innocence, beauty to the ever pure soul was only an image of God's beauty — an image which had descended from Heaven to rouse us up by its attraction to those celestial regions; it was also the mirror wherein the perfections of the innocent soul were visibly portrayed. Since the fall and consequent tendency of our minds towards what is low and base, beauty has become or may become a snare, and the Christian must learn to walk carefully along the brink of this precipice. No scrupulosity or over-straining is necessary; indeed, fearing a danger often provokes it, as fear of dizziness often brings on the very feeling. When the heart is simple and the intention upright, we may go boldly on, remembering the words of the Apostle — "To the pure all things are pure;"[1] and many a time, as Saint John Climacus, and before him other doctors, have remarked, the just man finds a subject of glory to God and a means of raising his soul to Him, where others find temptation and occasions of sin. This brings to my mind the idea of a moralist who wrote thus — "When I pick up shells and find pearls therein, I take out the pearls and throw away the shell."[2] Others, on the contrary, have a talent for casting away their pearls and keeping only the worthless shell, and sometimes the vase which holds it.

Again, "Beauty is vain," because, according to the observation of many philosophers, and the testimony of experience, it often happens that beauty is the inheritance of silly, weak women.[3] How else can it be, my children? Nature is not always an unjust stepmother, giving all to one child and withholding all from the others; no, there must be compensations awarded to plain people. I am far from asserting that ugliness is a cause or a condition of virtue; but it is a fact that many persons who are denied the possession of physical beauty are

---

[1] Titus 1:15.
[2] Pensées de Joubert, *titre prélim.*
[3] The Italians have a proverb — *Beltà et follia van spesso in compagnia.*

very rich in moral qualities, and have made much capital out of this fund. Their features have not the regularity, their complexion cannot boast that exquisite coloring, which forms what we call beauty in this world; but their minds are marvelously endowed; they are adorned with virtue, prudence, good sense, and judgment. All these interior qualities make up a nosegay, whose stems are within the heart, and whose flowers, blooming on the countenance, constitute in the eyes of a true observer a beauty far superior to that of the body — the beauty of a noble and upright soul, "which shows forth on the brow, and is perfumed like a flower from heaven."[1] And the Holy Ghost says — "As a golden ring in a swine's snout, so is a woman fair and foolish."[2]

Finally, beauty is vain, because, according to the beautiful remark of the Greek tragedian — "Beauty has never enabled a woman to retain her hold on her husband's heart, while virtue has been of the utmost efficacy to many."[3] No, my children, it is not beauty which keeps a heart constant; it may sustain the heart for a moment, but the chains are quickly thrown off if beauty be the sole attraction. God has set too high a value on the heart of man to permit it to yield the empire over itself completely and forever to so frivolous a thing as mere external beauty. Even if it wished to do so, the heart of man can never give itself up wholly thus; for it is endowed with superior instincts which react energetically; and these instincts will excite in it sentiments of shame and disillusion when he shall know the truth, and find there was nothing worthy of his affection behind that animated statue, whose whole wealth consisted of what the Scripture calls "deceitful favor and vain beauty." But that which really charms the heart of man, which attracts and fixes his affections, are the qualities of mind and heart; that gentle yet firm virtue, that unvarying sweetness, that untiring

---

[1] St Ambrose, *De Offic.* l. i. cap. xlv. t. iii. pp. 8, 9, edit Migné.
[2] Prov. 11:22.
[3] Euripides, cited by Saint Clement of Alexandria, *Stromat.* l. iv. cap. xx. p. 1338.

patience, that quiet fortitude in the misfortunes of life; and, before all, that profound religious feeling, that enlightened piety, whose practice is the safeguard and perfection of all a woman's best qualities, which elevates her character and her virtue to a height which nature, left to her own unaided powers, could never attain. A truly Christian woman is in her home "as a massive vessel of gold, adorned with every precious stone."[1] She is not a pretty toy intended to please for a day, nor merely a source of frivolous, perhaps sinful, relaxation; she is something holily beautiful, a sacred image of the goodness and loveliness of God; she is the vase of pure gold, whose metal shines the more brilliantly the more deeply it is wrought, and whose surrounding pearls are more precious because they form part of a massive and perfect whole. It is for such a woman, the model of true perfection, that the Holy Ghost reserves all His praises — "The woman that feareth the Lord, she shall be praised."

The Scripture adds — "Give her of the fruit of her hands: and let her works praise her in the gates." Give her of the fruit of her hands, that she may taste and enjoy in her turn all the good things she has produced; let her see her house prospering, her husband esteemed and respected, her children happy in their different paths of life, and her posterity extending themselves on all sides, like so many "...branches of honor and grace."[2] She shall enjoy the affection and consideration of all her family and of all persons who know her; above all, the poor, the sick, and the afflicted shall never pronounce her name but with a profound sentiment of gratitude and tender veneration; her remembrance shall be engraved in the hearts of all who have been forced to shed bitter tears, who have needed counsel and guidance, and to whom the alms of a sincere and heartfelt friendship have done so much good, especially at those moments in life when everything and every one seems to fail

[1] Ecclus. l:10.
[2] Ecclus. 24:22.

the poor exiled soul — "Give her of the fruit of her hands." Yes, give her to eat in the days of old age of those fruits so sweet and well flavored; none better are found on earth, and the terrestrial paradise itself might find somewhat to envy in that abundant harvest of the fruits of patience, self-devotion, tenderness, and mercy — divine fruits which can neither grow nor ripen where pain and suffering do not exist. Give, then, to this generous woman — give to her abundantly and above measure — the produce of the trees she has planted, and let their perfume be refreshment and marrow to her bones. "A good name maketh the bones fat."[1]

Let her works praise her in the assembly of the ancients; let her actions be a canticle of praise in her honor. The valiant woman does nothing in order to win praise; she does good for its own sake, and her intention is as pure as her self-sacrifice is sincere. Her God, the good of her family, and of her fellow-creatures has been her constant motto; and when the fame of her work has been bruited abroad, she has never willingly accepted more honor than was necessary for the edification and good example of others, according to the precept in the Gospel — "Let your light shine before men that they may see your good works and glorify your Father who is in heaven."[2] But our Lord, who has not the same motives for silence, wills that the good deeds of the valiant woman shall remain an enduring monument of her virtues — her conjugal tenderness, her maternal love, her charity towards the poor, her well-directed energy, her benevolence, and kindness towards all men. He wills that grave and venerable men, the judges as it were of the earth, shall point her out with respect to the present and future generations, saying — Behold the model of a woman, wife, and mother; contemplate this beauteous character, which has two sides apparently quite opposite, and yet which complete each other. On one hand, a womanly mind full of feminine delicacy, forethought, practical prudence, and

[1] Prov. 15: 30.
[2] St. Matt. 5:16.

gentleness; on the other, the vigorous intelligence of a man, with the resources, strength, energy, activity, and firm perseverance, which we admire in a masculine character — "And joining a man's heart to a woman's thought."[1]

I cannot better end these instructions than with those words from the Book of Machabees; they are the best, the simplest, and the most complete explanation of these two words which have been the theme of our discourses, and which contain a poem in action — THE VALIANT WOMAN. May mine not have been too feeble and unworthy a record of her glory and virtues! "Who shall find a valiant woman?"

---

[1] 2 Mach. 7:21.